"It is often another person's story that helps make sense of our own, and Nadine's is a powerful reminder of the brevity of life and the wonder of faith. This is a grace-filled memoir of joy on the gritty road of life and hope in the face of loss."

—Donna VanLiere, *New York Times* and *USA Today* bestselling author of *Finding Grace* and *The Christmas Shoes*

"People like Nadine motivate me. When I hear her story and see the great passion the Lord has given her for the people of Kosovo, I think: 'We need to help her! We need to support this God-breathed vision to the point where it can be unashamedly successful for Jesus Christ.'"

—Dr. Joseph Stowell, president of Cornerstone University, Grand Rapids, MI

"My wife and I had the privilege of watching Nadine grow in the Lord since she was a teenager. And, my oh my, what an amazing journey it's been. Seeing her story unfold and witnessing her love and dedication to Jesus Christ have been incredible blessings, not only for us, but also for the youth of Kosovo."

—Dr. Paul Dixon, former president of Cedarville University, Cedarville, OH

"Nadine's story bears all the distinguishing marks of a heart indelibly affected by Calvary's shadow and the glory of resurrection morning. To think of her spurs me forward. This is a story only God could write about a Savior's redemption, which only He could bring about."

—Dr. Eric Mounts, senior pastor of Bible Center Church, Charleston, WV

"*When You Don't See His Plan* is a very compelling story of God's work in and through the lives of an ordinary but committed family of believers. This is a story of love lived out in response to God's redeeming and sustaining love."

—Dr. Don Callan, retired athletic director, basketball coach, and founder of Missionary Internship Service, Cedarville University

"Never underestimate what God can do through a young woman's willing heart. Nadine's inspirational story will motivate you and encourage you to consider what God can do through you."

—Karol Ladd, author of *Power of a Positive Woman*, www.PositiveLifePrinciples.com

NADINE HENNESSEY
with REBECCA BAKER

The
Nadine
Hennesey
Story

WHEN YOU DON'T SEE HIS PLAN

DISCOVERY HOUSE
PUBLISHERS®

CONTENTS

ACKNOWLEDGMENTS

I can't say "thank you" enough to the mission teams whose investment of time and energy has helped Lydia and me keep going over the years. My mom, dad, brothers, and sisters have all been there for me—building, teaching, and coaching.

When we were in Albania, teams led by Pastor Scott Dewitt, Coach Don Callan, and missions director Brian Nester started an outreach that still continues.

Three weeks after Lydia and I arrived in Kosovo, a Cedarville University team led by photographer Scott Huck was here, helping with construction for the learning center. Other teams from my alma mater (Cedarville University), led by faculty and staff members such as Dave and Bev Robey, John and Ruth Hess, Cheryl Irish, Rebecca Baker, Dianna Nester, and Kristy Lester have taught classes and organized day camps. And friends from supporting churches have provided emotional, medical, and academic support.

One thing these teams have in common is that, although they may come in feeling like tourists, by the time they leave they are individuals who have made a difference. The kids love them, talk about them by name, and now, through e-mail and Facebook, often stay in contact. As one of them explained it to me recently, "once a House of Laughter family, always a House of Laughter family."

God has given me an amazing team of family and friends who have been a very valuable part of God's plan in my life. I thank God for my friendships that span thousands of miles.

I thank God for the prayer warriors who have prayed for me morning, noon, and night. I thank God for the sacrificial givers who continue to faithfully give of their resources in the midst of a struggling economy. I thank God for those who have traveled to Albania and Kosovo to work alongside me and for those who could not come, but gave so others could come. I thank God every time I think of each and every one of you.

—Nadine Hennesey

With deepest thanks to my husband, Wes, for supporting me, and to my friends and other family members for praying. Thank you, Pastor Eric Mounts, for bringing Nadine to our church where I first heard her story. And thanks to missions director Brian Nester, and world outreach minister Brent Miller, for encouraging me to travel to Kosovo. Thanks to my editor, Dave Branon, for patiently guiding the writing process. And Nadine, thank you for sharing your story and friendship. It's been a privilege coming alongside you!

—Rebecca Baker

INTRODUCTION

As I am writing at the desk in front of my apartment window, the sun's rays are warming the room. It's cold outside. The snow has lingered for several days. As I sit here, I notice my neighbor's yard. The side of the yard directly in the sun is a beautiful green. The side of the yard sitting in the shadow of the house is snow-covered.

Schools are closed today, so I am in my "empty nest"—trying to multi-task. A few moments ago, I put banana bread in the oven to take to my neighbors. I shouldn't do anything else when I'm baking, though; I've taken enough black-crusted bread out of the oven over the years to know that by now.

But here I sit writing lesson plans and thinking about people I love who live a long way away—in America.

Every day, I walk down the streets of Mitrovica, Kosovo. Ten years ago, when I came here, this was the flashpoint city between two cultures that were separated by a river, a bridge, and broken hearts. Today, a young, vital population is moving on. Walking among them are future leaders. "Someday," I have said, thinking about my students here in Kosovo, "someday one of them could be the prime minister . . . or the mayor . . . or the administrator of a new school."

"Teacher," many of the kids who run up and down the streets call me. Some because they've been my students and others just because that's how I'm known. I do have a name, but it doesn't really matter. I'm the American teacher who lives here, organizes crazy game nights, takes kids on skiing trips, makes them study really hard, and asks them to leave the room cleaner than they found it. You could be known for worse things. And some call me their second mom. You could hardly do better than that.

I didn't come here because it was a country where I always wanted to live. I started out on a journey of faith. The steps were by grace, as God gave me one good gift after another . . . although I didn't always see it at the time. But I love being part of life here. Most of all, I love the people. I'm home now.

I look out the window at my neighbor's yard—half green from the sun and half shadowed and covered with snow. And I think that it's easy to live in the shadow of our problems—the hard days, the misunderstandings, the tragedies. This country has been scarred. Devastation is still a matter of short-term memory; civil war a decade ago killed 10,000 people. But it's a new country. It needs leaders—leaders who have a vision for more than revenge, more than survival.

They need to know how to live in the light. We all do.

—Nadine Hennesey

1

OUT OF THE RUBBLE OF WAR—A DREAM

*"We were like those who dream,
then our mouth was filled with laughter."*
Psalm 126:1–2 (NKJV)

After a long, sleepless night, I finally gave up, got dressed, and slipped outside as the rising sun profiled buildings on the dusky horizon of Mitrovica. Just over two months earlier, this city in the tiny European territory of Kosovo had become my home. As an educator from the United States, I had come to join an international humanitarian team assisting survivors of the civil war that continued to tear the country apart. Even now I could peer through the early morning light and see a small helicopter perched on the hill behind us, guarding the site where a new building was being constructed—a learning center for kids who had, in a moment's time, lost childhood innocence as they witnessed family members being beaten or shot to death.

"We've been attacked," an American friend living nearby had called to tell me the day before, September 11, 2001. At first I thought she meant Kosovo was under siege—we were always alert to that possibility. "No," she responded, "the attack was in America." As soon as I heard that, I ran over to the guard's shack on our compound, struggling to understand the quick, terse news reports that kept coming in, spoken in Albanian.

I ran to find the nearest phone, and after repeated attempts over jammed phone lines, I connected with my parents in the States, who assured me they were safe.

Later that evening, the wife of our construction chief called. She was a doctor who specialized in blood work and was responding to the call to help American victims by organizing a couple of blood drives. If I wanted to come, she told me, she would pick me up early in the morning on her way into town. "I'll be ready," I assured her, thankful for the opportunity to do *something*.

So, on the morning of September 12, I had just stepped outside my apartment and was standing by the train tracks that edged our property when the young doctor pulled up. We drove past the marketplace, still quiet at that early hour, and entered the gate in front of an old military building that had been turned into a makeshift hospital.

Inside, even as the doctor was setting everything up, Albanian soldiers began coming in to donate blood. Steadily the line behind me grew until it extended out of the room, down the stairs, and outside. As we stood, waiting quietly together, I thought about the incredible carnage these soldiers and the citizens they served had lived through in the bloody struggle of the last three years. They had witnessed cold-hearted murder of fathers and brothers; some fearfully waited for the discovery of another mass grave that might reveal the remains of loved ones still missing. Every day's routine was marked by unavoidable reminders as the survivors walked past the places where friends or family had been killed. Many had lost their homes and any documents that gave them ownership rights to property. Yet, upon hearing news of thousands of injured Americans, these soldiers came, in sympathy and support, to give the only thing they could, their blood. Next to them, I felt small and insignificant.

After the first few of us in line had given blood, a man I assumed to be the men's commanding officer walked through the hallway, calling all the soldiers outside for a flag-raising ceremony. I slipped in behind and joined them. Standing on the dusty pathway circling the hospital, we came to attention as the Albanian and American flags were raised together, and then in honor of the 9-11 victims, the commanding officer called for a minute of silence. Although I had met this man at an event in town, I didn't think he would remember me, and I was humbled when he and his officers walked over, shook my hand, and expressed gratitude for America's support during Kosovo's recent political trauma.

Walking back home after the blood drive, I passed through Mitrovica's market area. Although I was out earlier than usual on this day, a quick walk to the city market had become part of my morning routine in Kosovo—one that let me meet people and connect with a growing network of friends. I usually slipped past groups of men sipping coffee at outdoor cafes as I headed toward one of my favorite bakeries for fresh croissants or rolls. Inevitably, a strong-spirited grandmother, her head wrapped in a scarf, would greet me with a kiss on both cheeks and whisper advice about the best places to shop. Young mothers dressed in more contemporary styles, without head coverings, would stop to talk, usually accompanied by little children who peeked up at me shyly. And older kids, walking arm-in-arm down the street, would run over to ask me about the new center being built near the train tracks.

"Teacher," they already called me. "Teacher, when does the center open?" At first, I didn't have an answer for their question. But after my best effort at diplomatic negotiation with my fellow administrators, we had finally committed to a date. "We'll open our doors on the fifteenth of September," I would promise those young people from then on.

But on this morning of September 12, I slipped into the marketplace with my eyes fixed on the sidewalk in front of me. To my surprise, someone coming toward me stopped suddenly. "Is your family safe?" he asked. A few moments later, another passerby touched my elbow. "We're so sorry," she said. As strangers and acquaintances continued to stop, echoing the unexpected support I had experienced at the hospital, I began to look around. I was touched by the sight of American flags draped in the windows of several stores and candles lit in others.

Mental images of devastation in America heightened my sensitivity to the political turmoil tearing Kosovo apart. As I did every morning, I passed the train tracks that came from beyond the bridge that separated the city into fiercely defined ethnic zones. Panic and terror could flare in an instant as Albanians and Serbians faced off in acts of war and revenge, resistance and survival.

I thought about the first time I saw the train coming our way carrying workers from "the other side." Little boys playing ball in the dirt nearby had been instantly galvanized into champions of their territory, running alongside the train leaving just enough distance to feel invulnerable, screaming angry obscenities accentuated with gestures of unmistakable intent. Recognizing some of the children from my visits in their homes added sad complexity to the scene, for this was more than "boys will be boys;" it was a change of persona. While unfiltered expressions of rage reflected what seemed to be a permanent emotional scar in some, for the most part these little boys looked different when you saw them up close in other settings. They loved to joke around, they were polite, and in rare moments of vulnerable self-disclosure, they were amazingly tenderhearted. I had already come to love them.

As I walked along the tracks that would lead back to where I had started that morning—the site of a new learning center rising out of the rubble of war—I thought about the dream that had led me to call this Eastern European city "home."

On July 5, 2001, while crossing the Albanian border into Kosovo on the way to my new adventure, I had traveled through a countryside banked with rugged mountains and dotted with one red-roofed house after another, all sitting empty. Initial framing of the houses had begun, but then they had been left unfinished. The job description I had been given was "to help orphans and semi-orphans in the war-torn city of Mitrovica, Kosovo." On a site visit the previous February to see what was at the time a pile of bricks bolstered by a big vision, this war-ravaged city had, against all odds, captured my heart. I wanted to make sure that I didn't leave my job unfinished.

During the two months since I arrived, as those bricks continued to rise out of the fragments of bombed-out buildings to form a learning center, I made countless home visits, accompanied by a translator. City officials had given me a list of more than seven hundred parents, mostly widows, who had lost spouses in the recent war. The devastation, vulnerability, and jagged loneliness I saw day after day haunted me. Beautiful, dignified women returned from refugee camps carrying children on their backs;

they struggled to rebuild lives in shattered fragments that had once been their homes.

For example, while visiting a temporary shelter that had been an old, condemned hotel, I heard a mother of six tell me how her children had been lined up and forced to watch as she and her husband were beaten. Leaving her husband lying on the ground, his torturers called out as they left, "You're not dead yet!" Wiping away her tears, she told what happened next. "My children tried to help me carry him to the hospital, but he died in my arms, in the street."

Another woman I visited, married the year before the war began, comforted the little one in her lap as she described the last night she had seen her husband alive. Soldiers had broken in, yanked the couple from their bed and through the front door, and set fire to the house. She watched, helpless, as they forced her husband to his knees with a gun to his back, and then they dragged him away. Fleeing across the river, she collapsed in an open field where, surrounded by wailing women and crying children, she gave birth in the pouring rain, not knowing if her baby would ever see his father. And now, she knew, he never would.

"What are your dreams for your children?" I would ask the survivors after they shared their stories. The same quick answer came again and again: "Education." Because local school buildings had been bombed and many teachers had been killed or injured, children could attend only the most salvageable facilities in half-day shifts, at best. Our learning center, I explained to these young mothers, would be available to orphaned and semi-orphaned children as a supplement to the local public school programs.

My goal was to hire four Albanian teachers, and together we would offer classes in literature, math, English, art, and character training. Two cooks would use the kitchen and dining room to provide a nourishing lunch each day. And because of the vital role athletics play in teaching discipline, fostering teamwork, and building character, I had also lobbied our vision team for a sports facility. "These kids need a place for organized activity," I shared with my team. "More than that, they desperately need a place other than the streets—a safe place—where they can hang out and play."

The response was enthusiastic but conditional. Could I raise the extra money needed, they asked, to supplement the already stretched budget? That night I wrote to my supporters back in the States, promising to mention the request only once and trust God for the result. Just as construction needed to begin, my mission organization confirmed contributions that had come in, including one for $30,000 from a friend in my home church. The total at the bottom of the column was exactly what was needed!

During a lunch break one August day, after coming back from an especially disheartening home visit, I sat in the shade of a tree on the edge of our property and took a hard look at how we were progressing. The sun was scorching. We still had to carry water into the kitchen and bathroom every day, the construction workers were exhausted, and, most troubling to me personally, I wondered if we could make a dent in the grief surrounding us. After eating the bit of bread and cheese I had taken outside with me, I opened my Bible to Psalm 126:1–2. "We were like those who dream," it began. "Then our mouth was filled with laughter."

The House of Laughter, I thought, looking up at the construction, which had slowed down lately. I thought of the frightened, fragile little girl I had visited that morning. Her little brother, trying hard to act tough, obviously craved attention; her older brother didn't even attempt to disguise his anger as he sat with arms crossed, glaring at everyone in the room. What would it take to see them laugh? More than a building, I thought. More than games, books, and food—or anything *we* could offer even on our best days. I looked back at the Bible in my lap and read the next verse. "The Lord has done great things for us." Thankful that grace from heaven isn't limited by earthly resources, I put a marker at that place, and the next day proposed The House of Laughter as the name for our learning center. My administrators looked at each other, smiled, and turning back to me, nodded their approval.

My dream—that these besieged people of Kosovo could know the joy that only God could give—was one that had grown from seeds planted in my heart many years before. The way I had been raised played a big part in leading me to my new home in the middle of Eastern Europe. My parents had lived out their faith in practical ways. The compassion I saw in them meant getting your hands dirty and your heart broken for needs beyond your own. In the few moments we are given in this short life, we earn the opportunity to put our arms around someone else and help. And I had learned firsthand from my dad, who turned every project into a game, that if you give people a chance to laugh it's a lot easier for them to get up and move on.

On September 15, 2001, I woke up, asked God for His will to be done, and watched as the dream of laughter came into focus.

With pale, yellow paint barely dry on classroom walls and desks delivered just the day before, The House of Laughter was officially dedicated in a public program. Dressed as clowns, one of my teachers, Stacey, and her little helper—a young girl named Lydia—passed out balloons as visitors came through the gate. Standing outside our new building, single-parent families, friends, and reporters from the newspaper and radio station gathered around the mayor of Mitrovica, who cut the ribbon and welcomed us as an official part of the city. Although no American soldiers were allowed to attend because of the high-alert status still in effect, international soldiers in full uniform mingled with the crowd, joining in the celebration.

During the reception that followed, I slipped into my office for a moment of private celebration. Over my desk hung a poster I brought from the United States. It showed smiling children of many nationalities circling a globe, with these words: "Teachers change the world—one child at a time." "Please, Lord," I prayed, "please work through me, in any way you choose, to change their world."

I heard muffled laughter and glanced up to see three young girls standing arm in arm outside my office window, obviously *trying* to wait respectfully. "Mom, come back to the party!" the little clown helper in the middle called, jumping up and down.

"I'll be right there." The girls ran back to their friends, and I turned to join them, stopping momentarily to straighten the photos on the shelf across from my desk. There was one of my husband and me at our wedding, another of our family taken at Christmas, and one in a silver heart of the ten-year-old girl who had just called me "Mom."

The path that led me from a supportive home in the farmlands of Ohio to war-torn Kosovo was not one I could have foreseen nor one which, humanly speaking, I would have chosen. It was only God's grace that brought Lydia and me here. And that grace, I knew, was enough.

I knew.

2

THE WAY WE WERE

"Each day of our lives we make deposits
in the memory banks of our children."
—Charles Swindoll

My parents spent time with us when we were growing up. My dad, Doug Terrill, was a builder who put in long days, but he always played with us when he came home. He would do things like take the cushions off the couch and pretend we were riding horses. Or he would turn the dining room table into a landing base for our paper airplanes.

I didn't realize it back then, but my mom, Linda, had a ton of work to do in caring for all of us. I was born three weeks before her twentieth birthday, and within seven years she had five children. Much later, when I was in high school, my youngest brother came along. We had lots of friends, but it was in our family that we had our very best friends. When I think of what "family" is supposed to mean, I think of my family: The Terrills of Xenia, Ohio.

One of my most vivid childhood memories was April 3, 1974, when tragedy struck our hometown. Dad was working in his office in the basement that day, and the three of us older girls were watching *Gilligan's Island* on the television in our living room. My mother had just put the four-month-old twins, Troy and Sheri, down for naps.

Mom asked me to keep an eye on them while she made a quick trip to the meat store. Then she was going to stop by our church to arrange the elements for Sunday's communion service. About halfway into our program, just after the words "Tornado Warning" flashed across the TV screen, my mom suddenly threw open the front door. "Run downstairs!" she yelled as Dad raced up the stairs to see what was happening. "We could see the tornado forming through the window at church!" Mom exclaimed as she ran from the twins' bedroom, one baby under each arm. "I got in the car and came right home, and I could see our neighbors outside, watching."

We scampered down to the basement, where Dad and Mom put all of us under the ping-pong table. Then they ran back upstairs to look outside. A few minutes later they were back with us, and they reported that the sky was black and the roof shingles of the neighbor's house were being blown straight up into the air. We huddled together listening to what sounded like a freight train racing overhead.

When the noise died down, we crept upstairs to the living room and opened the front door. Our house and the ones immediately around us were still standing, but circling further out, fallen trees were tossed in with chaotic piles of shingles, bricks, and shattered glass.

One of the most massive tornados in US history had just devastated Xenia. It was later discovered to have been an F5 tornado, perhaps the most violent kind. Thirty-four people in our community died that day, and the tornado did millions and millions of dollars in damage.

We found out later that one family in our church had all crammed together into a closet. When they opened the door after the tornado passed, they discovered that the whole house was gone—except the closet.

I was eight years old at the time, and I look back on that day as my first recognition of life's uncertainty. We had neighbors come stay with us that night, and with no electricity, we sat around the table listening to a battery-operated radio. As reports of missing people were updated, we heard that the little boy my sister sat next to in first grade had been killed. With the severity of this tornado, we began to realize that though the death count was rising, many more could have been killed. One startling report we heard later was that a school bus parked outside Xenia High School had been picked up and dropped onto the school stage where, minutes before the warning, students had been practicing a play.

The next day we drove to the airport, and Dad put us on a plane so we could stay with my Aunt Patricia and Uncle Lee in Georgia. After checking with our pastor, Bill Wheeler, to find out which families in the church and community had suffered the greatest damage, Dad got to work. For the next three weeks, he volunteered night and day, cleaning up debris, beginning reconstruction on houses that could be salvaged, and finding shelter for friends who had lost their homes completely.

"Every job can be a ministry," Dad's college president, Dr. James T. Jeremiah, had counseled him years earlier when Dad said he needed to drop out of school because his first child was on the way. Dad had been taking classes toward a Bible degree at Cedarville University, a Christian liberal arts school just a few miles east of Xenia. He paid his bill by working construction on campus. He had just helped transform a former Presbyterian church into the school's basketball gymnasium. Dad never went back to school and never became a pastor—but watching him after the tornado and in other situations, I've seen Dr. Jeremiah's wisdom become reality.

Because Dad made a living by working in construction, the state of the economy meant more to us than just a newspaper headline. When a recession hit the nation while we were growing up, we felt it every day. One night, after going without a contract for weeks, Dad shared our need during family devotions.

"I don't want this to go beyond us," he began, "but we need to pray about how we'll get groceries this week." We prayed but told no one—just as he asked. That Sunday night we came out of church and opened the door of our van to discover that it had been filled with bags of groceries. At home as we unloaded the bags, Mom found an envelope, opened it, and without a word passed it to Dad. There was $200 in cash in the envelope—an anonymous gift.

Another night close to Christmas, Dad apologized for being short on spending money after paying the bills. "I don't think we can take our trip to New York to see your grandparents," he began. When we pressed him for details, he opened his wallet and pulled out twelve dollars.

"That's it. After gas, that's all we have for the trip."

We talked it over, packed a cooler with food, and took off anyway. We stopped to play football at rest stops for entertainment, and we got to New York and back with a little money to spare. It was one of the best vacations we ever had!

Dad was a natural coach. When I started attending Xenia Christian High School, there wasn't a girls' basketball team, so Dad asked if he could put one together. We looked like a ragged bunch of rookies on opening day of practice, but Dad never let on. He was a drill sergeant and our number one supporter—all wrapped into one. "Never, *never* give up" was the motto he challenged us with so consistently we could have printed it on our team shirts. To everyone's amazement (especially ours), at the end of our first season we won the Middletown Christian Invitational. Middletown had beaten us twice during the season, and coming into the tournament we were definitely the underdogs.

In our second season we won the Association of Christian Schools International state championship for our division. With less than thirty seconds on the clock of the championship game, we were down by one point. Dad called our last time-out, motioned us to the sidelines, and sketched out a strategy. As we ran back onto the court, he grabbed my arm. "If you're going to win this, you've got to do it *now*." Intercepting the ball, I dribbled down the court and made a lay-up. As our opponent geared up to take the lead back in the closing seconds, my sister, Tami, repeated the play with a steal and lay-up of her own. As the buzzer sounded the scoreboard showed that we had won the championship game by three points! Tami told me afterward that if I could do it, she knew she could too.

If Dad was a great coach, Mom was our faithful cheerleader. She navigated through bats, balls, gloves, nets, rackets, skates, and skateboards. And that was just getting out of the garage into the driveway. But our constant activity continually tested her desire to keep even a semblance of order inside the house. One night after supper, Dad asked us to wait a minute before we started clearing the table. "Your mom says we tear around in here too much," he began.

"I didn't say that exactly, Doug," Mom interjected.

"I have an idea," Dad continued. "Let's build a barn. My office and workshop will be on the ground floor. And then we can use the top floor for whatever you want. I was thinking maybe a—"

"A basketball court!" we shouted unanimously.

"Okay. If we all work together, we can build it this summer."

By mid-summer our office/workshop/sports barn was finished, basketball court and all. There were bars on the windows to protect the glass and shields on the lights. My dad had made toys for us when we were little and just kept making bigger ones as we grew up. He added a slide outside the second floor window of the barn and a swing hanging from the ceiling in the middle of the court that almost reached the basket if you worked it just right. I spent hours practicing until I could swing, holding a basketball between my knees. At just the right height, I would release the ball, letting it roll down my legs. Then I would catch it between my feet. Slam dunk! I could slam dunk the basketball with my feet!

From then on, we spent our summers playing outside as long as we could. But in the winter, we headed into the barn. On the coldest days of the year, even though we could see our breath and had to blow on our hands, we kept playing. We planned lots of activities for friends at school and our church youth group, but even when it was just us, we would hurry to finish schoolwork and jobs around the house so we could run into our sports barn and play together.

Being fiercely competitive, laughing at our mistakes, and pushing each other past what was comfortable were all parts of the family value package I grew up with.

Sometimes this tendency I inherited for that tenacity feels more like stubbornness. My mom kindly attributes it to my July 4 birthday, and she calls it my "independent spirit." I was born with a condition that resulted in weakened ankle tendons and ligaments. My feet turned in, and I had to wear leg braces for a year. The metal rods went down from a belt to my shoes, and there were straps around my knees. I didn't feel sorry for myself—no one would let me—but I remember how great it felt when the braces came off when I was five. From then on, I pushed myself to ride my bike or run faster than anyone else, even though I wasn't always watching where I was going. One time I was trying to help round up some horses that got loose from the neighbor's yard. Running as fast as I could alongside a horse, I slammed right into the barbed wire fence.

It's true. As a kid I earned a reputation for jumping into things with both feet but not my brain. For example, I volunteered to play "The Stars and Stripes Forever" as the other junior high students marched in for our spring program. Although this was far beyond my first grade John Thompson piano lessons, I was sure I could conquer the piece. As my hands shook uncontrollably, no one could even recognize the song, and I knew my parents must have disappeared somewhere under their seats.

And I still have to live with the stories my younger brothers and sisters tell of the times I made dinner when my folks would have a rare night out. Admittedly, my cavalier attitude about the ingredients may have had something to do with the groans at the table when dinner was served. "No tomato sauce?" I said to myself one night as I began, reading Mom's recipe for lasagna. "Not a problem—I'll use the homemade chili instead." Actually, the only ingredient listed that I had to work with was the noodles. For hamburger, I scrounged around until I found something close, sort of . . . pepperoni. Turning up their noses as my version of what had always been a family favorite came out of the oven, Troy and Tami said it didn't *smell* like lasagna. "It doesn't even *look* like lasagna," Cindy added as Sheri shook her head. "You eat it," they all said together. Even our dog walked away when I put some in his dish. I grabbed a fork and took a big bite. Then we called out for pizza.

As a young girl, though, I knew that some decisions called for the use of my head as well as my heart. As a junior in high school, I described in my journal the man I wanted to marry—if I married. "It doesn't really matter what he looks like," I began, and added, "though it would be nice if he's tall, dark, handsome, and athletic. What does matter is that he loves God with all his heart and cares about people more than things. He should have a great sense of humor, should respect his parents, and should love children. And being with him should make me want to be a better person."

Although I kept these details to myself, my family and friends knew there was an elusive perfect guy out there for me. He became affectionately known to all of us as "Mr. Right." If I really didn't want to date a guy someone suggested, I wouldn't have to explain why. "He's just not Mr. Right," I would say. My best friend, Cindy Baise, caught on to this and told me she didn't think there really was such a guy. I told her there was and in fact, his first name was Peter. I liked the strong will of Peter in the Bible, and the name stuck—Peter Right.

"Hi, I'm Peter Wright," a young man said as he introduced himself to our class one Sunday morning at Calvary Baptist Church, "but most people call me Pete." He was a broadcasting major at Cedarville, he said, and he was just visiting. This was nothing unusual, I thought, as I wondered why I was getting funny looks from all my friends. Then his name sank in: Peter Wright! I bit my lip and looked straight ahead, but inside I was laughing so hard the pew shook. He seemed like a nice guy, and his first name was Peter, but he wasn't my Mr. Right.

In the years since I have officially grown up and have begun navigating life's hard times of confusion and despair, memories of home have rescued me. As I've wondered how to help kids who act out their anger by using the only coping strategies they know—hitting harder and screaming louder—I hear a coach's voice in the back of my mind. "Work as a team . . . don't give up." As I've sat in budget meetings, wondering if it's crazy to dream of great things when available funds suggest we should quit, scenes of family trips that were short on money but tall on good times come to mind. When communicating with people from other cultures has thrown me a challenging curve ball, I celebrate the language of humor we all share. And when circumstances have been so overwhelming I want to give up, I remember all the nights our family gathered to pray. "Faith is trust followed by action," are words my grandmother passed on to all of us.

"If you're going to win this, you've got to do it now," my dad said as he sent me back into our championship basketball game in high school. Those same words have echoed in my thoughts often.

Even when it seemed I had everything to lose.

3

LOVE, GRACE, AND MARRIAGE

*"There is no more lovely, friendly, charming relationship,
communion, or company than a good marriage."*
—Martin Luther

Our church was small, so when anyone new walked through the door everyone noticed. It wasn't any different when Edson Hennesey walked through the doors that snowy January morning in 1987. Ed, as everyone called him, was not one to sit around and wait for things to happen. He connected quickly, participating in workdays, volunteering to do yard work for the widows, leading the singing on Sunday mornings, and joining the men's softball league. We became casual friends as we participated in the College and Career class, and in various other activities in the church. Casual, that is, until after my college graduation.

It was a busy week. My sister, Cindy, had just graduated from Xenia Christian High School, and I was handed my diploma from Cedarville University's president, Dr. Paul Dixon, that beautiful Saturday morning, June 6, 1987. To celebrate the week's events, my parents planned a double open house for Cindy and me Sunday night after church. There was an open invitation to the entire church, and as I headed out the door for the party after our evening service, Ed stopped me.

"Congratulations!" he said. And then he casually asked if I would like to watch the church league softball game the next night.

I didn't tell him I would rather play than watch. I can't even sit still long enough to watch a Major League game on television, and as much as I appreciated the men in our church . . . Instead of telling him all that, I simply said, "Sure, I'd like to come."

"Great," he said. "I'll pick you up."

After the game the following evening, Ed asked me if I wanted to go get some ice cream before he took me home. Ever since my senior year in high school, I had cut sweets out of my diet to help my speed on the basketball court. Should I set that aside to go with his suggestion, I wondered for a moment? But I decided to be honest, and I told Ed I didn't eat ice cream.

"That's okay," he said right away. "I have another idea." He stopped at a small grocery store, ran in, and bought some sweet cherries.

It was a beautiful June evening. We rolled down the car windows and rather than driving straight to my house took the longer road through the countryside. From the very start we felt a friendly competition with each other. I don't think I would have ever done this with anyone else—after all I hardly knew the guy—but at some point we started laughing and spitting cherry seeds out the windows, which led to seeing whose seeds could hit the mailboxes we passed. Of course, I couldn't resist the challenge. When I thought about it later that night, it was striking how comfortable we were just enjoying being ourselves—how it felt like a mutual decision to not try to impress each other.

The next day we went for a bike ride together. As we rode side-by-side down the road and then stopped to eat, we talked about family, sports, school, ambitions, and what we really cared about in life. That's when I realized how many of our goals matched, and as hard as I tried to ignore them, the words "Peter Right" kept coming to mind.

Ed had received his one-year degree from Word of Life Bible Institute, and he graduated in 1985 from Tennessee Temple University in Chattanooga, Tennessee, with a history degree. While in school he helped with a local church youth ministry. I told him how my advisor, Dr. Sharon Eimers, and other Cedarville education professors had shaped my vision for working with children facing difficult circumstances. I explained that with the encouragement of my Fundamentals of Speech professor, Dr. David Robey, I pushed myself out of my comfort zone and traveled with the intercollegiate speech team, although I was definitely the fledgling among pros. And I told Ed about my part in *For This Cause*, Dr. Robey's play about John and Betty Stam, who gave their lives as missionaries in China.

When I asked Ed about his family, he told me about his older brother, Jack (who had been named after their dad), their younger sister, Gwen, and his mother Barbara. "Mom's an incredible woman who means everything to me," he said. Then he shared how, eight years earlier, his schoolteacher father had died unexpectedly. Ed was fifteen at the time, he told me. A junior in high school.

"My mom and I had just arrived at the hospital waiting room when we heard the code blue alert and rushed into my father's room. When my dad recovered for a few moments, we were standing by his bed. He looked at my mother and told her he loved her and each of us kids. Then he added what turned out to be his last words, 'And I love Jesus.' " That was a comfort, Ed explained, because though he had shared his faith with his father, he had never been sure of his dad's response.

"My mom assured us she wanted all of us to go on with our plans for college," Ed told me, "but Jack and I felt that one or the other of us should live at home at least until Gwen graduated from high school." Ed explained that Jack worked while he went to Tennessee Temple. Then Ed came back home so Jack could finish college. Ed worked for three semesters as a substitute teacher in the same school in which his dad had taught. When Gwen told the family she was engaged to be married to George, her high school sweetheart, Ed told me, he felt the time was right to pick up his plans to follow his dream of missions in Peru, and he enrolled at Cedarville for further training in Spanish.

After our bike ride Ed asked if I would like to play tennis on Saturday. Besides challenging each other athletically, we decided to add a spiritual challenge. Ed was working on memorizing 1 Timothy, and I wanted to memorize the book of James. We planned to quote the first chapters after the tennis match.

"Three dates in one week," my sister, Tami, mentioned casually as we cleared the table after dinner on Friday evening. Then she added that people were beginning to talk about how well suited Ed and I were for each other.

"Who said that?" I asked.

"Oh, people at church," Tami said. "Well, everybody who knows the two of you."

I knew it wouldn't take long for the matchmaking to begin, so I devised a plan to indirectly let Ed know we needed to slow down. I had to get the situation back under control.

The next day when we played tennis, I let Ed see my competitive side in full swing. I totally creamed him. But this didn't bother him, apparently, and when we got to my house he stayed to play a little basketball with my brother, Troy. During a break, Ed came into the house, sat down, and asked me to quote James 1. No problem. I was ready. I rattled off the chapter as I made a pineapple smoothie. "You made nine mistakes," he declared when I finished. "You said 'a' instead of 'the' in verse six . . ."

"What!?" I didn't let him finish. This is when my pride stepped in. "You mean you sat there counting every mistake I made! Give me the Bible. It's your turn. Quote 1 Timothy 1."

"Nadine, I didn't count the mistakes to make you mad," he said. "God's Word is the most precious possession we have on this earth. We should do our very best when memorizing it and using it. You have the ability to memorize God's Word perfectly. You should do it."

Ed's words did not change my attitude. "Say 1 Timothy 1," I ordered. I was ready to count every pause that was not in the right place. To my frustration, he said it without a mistake.

Apparently, my attempt to slow things down didn't work, and a few days later the phone rang. It was Ed. He wanted to know if I would go out with him the next day.

I turned him down.

"You're so stubborn," my sister said over her shoulder as she walked by.

"I know exactly what I'm doing," I shot back. And I did. By then I had really fallen for the guy. It wasn't a matter of what people were saying anymore. It was me. I felt sure this was a sign of weakness on my part after knowing him such a short time.

In mid-August I started teaching and coaching volleyball at Xenia Christian. It would have been hard to find a free moment to see Ed, anyway, I kept telling myself as the weeks rolled past without any contact with him. By the time four months had gone by since Ed had last asked me out, I had to admit to totally messing up a good thing. "If you want us together, Lord, please let him ask me out tomorrow," I prayed, putting the mess I had made into God's hands. "If not, well, that will be the end of this chapter, and I'll go on."

The next evening we had choir practice at church, and Ed sat directly behind me. Before practice started he leaned forward. "Say," he ventured, "now that your volleyball season is finished and you've got a little more time . . . I was wondering if you'd like to go with me to Word of Life's performance, *Revelation*, tomorrow night."

"Let me check my schedule," I said looking at my calendar and knowing full well I was free Monday night. "Yes, I guess I'm free."

Some things in life we plan, I was beginning to see, and others simply come by grace, grace that is greater than being guided by circumstances, or in my case, stubbornness.

My parents hadn't talked much about their dating relationship while we were young, but I heard enough to know that they too had seen God's special guidance.

My dad was raised on a farm in upstate New York. His mother, Mabel, was a Methodist minister who raised her family "by the book," in more ways than one.

My mother was born to a single girl of seventeen who dropped out of school when she discovered she was pregnant. Although the young father helped pay the hospital bill, he said his parents wouldn't let him get married.

When my mom was a year old, her mother married another man. Four years after that, she divorced him, and she married again three years later. Two little brothers came along by the time Mom was a teenager, and she did her best to take care of them after school. She made supper each night while her mother went to work. Meanwhile, the second stepfather often came home drunk and was abusive. "My mother was a beautiful young woman, and I loved her," my mom confided in me, "but she never regained her confidence after being mistreated by her husband. I grew up following them from bar to bar."

As a high school junior, my mother, who had been in church some but with little personal connection, decided to use the weekly release time offered by her school to take a class at a little church down the street. That's how she heard about Jesus, and one day she asked Him to be her Savior. "I still don't know much about religion," she told one of her teachers later, "but I think I made a big decision today."

That summer, she stayed with her Aunt Irene, who lived near Mabel Terrill. It didn't take long for Aunt Irene to arrange a visit timed so that they would just happen to be visiting when Mabel's son, Doug, came home from baseball practice. That summer my mom and dad became friends, and during the next year he often went to visit her family. His kindness to her little brothers was the quality that touched her most. "I knew by then I wanted a man who loved God, loved children, and would be a good father," my mom told me as she related their story.

My parents had been led down very different paths to meet and fall in love. In the same way God's grace brought them together, He worked to salvage the mess I had made with the man I already knew I loved. From the night we went to the Word of Life program, my heart belonged to Ed. I couldn't stop thinking about him. When I was finishing my school day, Ed was starting his workday at another small Christian school in Xenia. On his way from his classes at Cedarville to his janitorial job at the school, he would stop and leave a creative message or a little snack for me in my car. Then when my school day was over, I would sneak out as quickly as possible to enjoy the treasure he had left me. It didn't take long for my seventh and eighth grade students to realize what was happening, and they devised a little plan. One day a couple of students detained me in the classroom with a history question while the others dashed for my little red Nova to read the "sweet mushy message" before I could get to it.

"And that is why car locks were invented," I explained to my science class the next day with a grin. "To keep your inquisitive minds where they need to be."

Creativity was a gift Ed and I developed during our dating relationship, because we had very little money. The first Christmas, we agreed to spend no more than three dollars on each other. I crocheted a scarf for Ed, my one and only completed attempt at this needlecraft to this day. Ed used it as a runner for his dresser. For Ed's gift for me, he worked out a secret arrangement with my parents, who gave him a key to our house before our family left for New York to visit my grandma and grandpa. When we returned, we found a cardboard miniature shopping mall, crafted from a refrigerator box, in the middle of the living room. Next to it was a note from Ed, welcoming us home, and a cassette tape player with recorded Christmas carols to play while we shopped. In the appropriate store for each member of the family, there was a little, inexpensive gift. The last stop was the music store, where there was to be a gift for me. When I had told Ed earlier that I really wanted a guitar but couldn't afford one, he had hinted about one he had, and I couldn't wait to see if this was what waited inside the music store. It was empty, though. Ed called later that night to explain that, after coming back from visiting his family in Michigan, he realized he had forgotten to bring back the guitar! "Can I give it to you later?" he asked.

But Ed was way ahead in planning another gift for me. On June 6, he and I said goodbye as our family took off for a six-week camping vacation from Ohio to Alaska and back. When I opened my duffel bag that night, I discovered a card from Ed. And the next day I found another. Ed had given a stack of cards to my sister Tami to hide—one for every day of our trip. Inside each one, he had written a personal note followed by a Bible verse—with the idea that he and I could read and reflect on it together. Every morning of the trip I would get away by myself, read that day's card, and pray. One morning as I sat on a crest looking out over the Grand Canyon, I realized that the more I fell in love with Ed, the more I was falling in love with God as well.

The following school year Ed accepted a position teaching Spanish at Hollywood Christian School near Fort Lauderdale, Florida. He also arranged to assist at the Primera Iglesia Bautista Hispana—a Spanish-speaking church—while I continued teaching in Xenia. It was difficult saying goodbye, but we looked ahead to seeing each other over Christmas break. For Christmas 1988 we each decided to plan something fun we could do as our gift to each other.

Ed joined my family in New York to celebrate, so I surprised him with his special Christmas gift activity. We left the house at six in the morning. I thought it would be romantic to eat a picnic breakfast as we watched the sun rise from a beautiful spot where hang gliders jumped. It was a tough climb getting to that spot up the steep mountain, in two feet of snow, carrying a picnic basket. When we finally arrived, heaving for breath and sweaty, I walked out to the ledge to take in the beautiful scene. I wasn't going to let the fact that the wind chill factor was 20 below zero spoil our special moment. The entire time I was pouring my heart out to Ed as I stood on the ledge—only to realize after a short while that he wasn't there. I found him huddled behind a tree. He was the practical one in our relationship. And that's not a bad quality, I thought as we romantically ate our breakfast behind the tree and quickly headed home to thaw out.

We drove to Michigan to spend time with his family. Ed took me to Germantown in Detroit for what I thought to be his special event, but he had another surprise waiting for me. Ed had been praying, thinking, and seeking counsel about the future of our relationship. He valued the wisdom of his mother, and earlier that year they had stayed up late talking about marriage. "When do you know it's right?" he asked her.

"When she means more to you than you mean to yourself," she answered. "And when you would do anything—or give up anything—for her." That's when Ed decided it was time to get my dad's permission to propose to me.

Ed and I were staying with his sister, Gwen, and her husband, George, at their house on Lake Huron. Early in the morning on December 29, 1988, Ed asked me if I would walk with him along the lake. Of course I would, I said, especially after he had been willing to climb a mountain at six in the morning for me. We walked along the shore shivering in the cold and sharing memories. Ed asked me to sit on an old piece of driftwood. He knelt on one knee and asked me to marry him. "Yes," I answered quickly, assuredly. He put the ring on my finger, and we ran as fast as we could back to the house to get warm.

Ed left to finish his school year in Florida after Christmas, and we wrote to each other six days a week. One big part of our future was becoming clear. Ed's work with the Spanish-speaking people in his school and church confirmed the passion he had shared with me earlier to go to Peru as a missionary. He was considering applying to Dallas Theological Seminary to finish preparation. As a friend, I had supported his dream. Now as his fiancée, I was excited to think of us living it out as a couple. Whatever we did, I told him, the best part was that we would be together. "It's hard being apart now," Ed wrote to me one night, "but I'm glad that when we're married, we—most likely—will not have to face that trial."

On July 1, 1989, Ed and I were married in an outdoor ceremony behind my family's home in Xenia. The song we chose to play as we walked down the aisle, Steve Green's recording of "Find Us Faithful," reflected the desire we committed to for life.

Maybe because of our strong personalities, we had promised to never go to bed angry with each other. I had heard that the first year of marriage might be a real struggle of adjusting to one another, but somehow we bypassed that. We were more than husband and wife—we were best friends, companions, and lovers—and I can honestly say that we were adjusted by the time we said, "I do."

Ed Hennesey was exactly who I had been looking for.

4

"SEE YOU FOR LUNCH?"

"I decided I need to make the most of every day
—from the minute I wake up."
—Ed Hennesey's college journal

If being newlyweds means working hard all day to pay the bills, we fit the definition perfectly. If it means ending the day by walking somewhere—anywhere—just to be together and to talk for hours because we had so much to say to each other, that's what we were. And if it means being madly in love, we were as newlywed as you could be even as one month of married life slipped into the next. Every night as I fell asleep next to Ed, I thanked God for another happy day.

Hollywood, Florida, was our first home. We moved there right after we were married. Ed worked construction all week so we could be a part of the Primera Iglesia Bautista Hispana, the church where he had interned the year before. On Sundays he led the singing, and I did my best at the piano. At least they didn't ask me to play "Stars and Stripes Forever."

My Spanish, of course, wasn't as good as Ed's, and many times I would start playing the wrong hymn, having misunderstood the page number he announced. Ed would smile and wait until I found my place. "Getting the numbers correct now," he told me, "will make life easier for you when we get to Peru."

While living in Florida, in the early spring of 1990 we got a phone call from Ed's best friend, Tim Collard, who pastored their home church near Port Huron, Michigan.

"Would you consider letting me put in your name for interim youth minister?" Tim asked. Ed told him that we were applying to a mission board and might be able to stay for only one year. "Perfect," Tim responded. "It would be great to work together until you're ready to go to Peru."

So, at the end of April we packed up our stuff and moved from Florida to Goodells, Michigan, which was still home to my husband's family. We settled our few belongings into a little apartment down the street from the church.

Ed's mother, Barbara, and her new husband, Bruce Witherspoon, invited us to their house often. Grilling out in their backyard almost always turned into a big family get-together with nieces, nephews, and cousins joining in. As I slipped into the picture, watching all of them eating and playing crazy games together, I got glimpses of what growing up must have been like for my husband. It was a gift I never expected.

Being in Michigan also meant being closer to my parents than when we were in Florida. On Memorial Day my family came from Ohio to share the long weekend with us and to celebrate another gift that had come as a pleasant surprise to Ed and me.

I was pregnant!

As soon as we found out I was expecting, right around Easter, Ed thought of a great way to tell my parents. He called Millie and Margie—two widow ladies from my home church in Xenia—

and asked them a favor. They had taken Ed under their wing while he lived in Xenia, so he knew they would come through. Would they buy a floral arrangement in a special vase, he asked—one designed to celebrate a new baby—and give it to my parents that Sunday? Along with money for the flowers, we sent a card to put with them—including a little poem I had written announcing that my mom and dad were going to be grandparents.

We were now less than one month away from our first wedding anniversary. Right after Memorial Day, as I was beginning the second trimester of pregnancy, Ed went with me to the doctor's office where, together, we heard our baby's heartbeat for the first time.

Life was sweet, I thought, snuggling back against my pillow on June 6—just five days after hearing the heartbeat. "Good morning, Hon," Ed said, turning off the alarm at seven o'clock. He brushed back my hair and kissed my forehead. "Hard night?" he asked. "I heard a lot of tossing and turning."

"It's just this cold," I answered. "If it weren't for that, I'd be fine."

"Well, stay in bed and get some more sleep if you can," he said as he tucked the covers back around me. "You need your rest right now."

For a few minutes I could hear Ed in the kitchen, opening the refrigerator to pull out the apple cinnamon pancakes I had made the day before. Then I drifted into the best sleep I'd had for a long time. I didn't wake up until the phone rang at 8:36.

Ed came in the room a few moments later and sat on the side of the bed as he put his shoes on. He told me that the phone call was from my friend, Sandy Collard, who wanted to know if I felt like going shopping with her that morning.

"I told her you were resting but would call her back soon," he said.

He glanced at his watch. "Gotta go, Hon," he said. "We're planning the biking trip for the youth group today." Then he lay down on the bed and wrapped his arms around me. And, as he had done every morning since he first heard the baby's heartbeat, Ed kissed my tummy and whispered, "Daddy loves you." He hugged me again and pulled the covers over my shoulders. At the door he turned back and smiled. "Will I see you for lunch?"

"Of course." Taking lunch to eat with Ed in his office had, by then, become a favorite part of my daily routine. "It might be a little later than usual, though."

"Take your time, sweetheart. I love you."

I listened as Ed bounded down the stairs. Just like always.

It was nearly 1:00 by the time I got back home after shopping with Sandy and her children. In our small kitchen I could reach from the refrigerator to the counter and back again without taking a step. Less than five minutes later, with lunch in hand—chicken salad sandwiches and some apple cobbler left from dessert the night before—I headed out the door.

First Baptist Church of Goodells was just down the street. As I walked that way I could see Pastor Tim, taking his lunch break with Sandy and the kids in the front yard of their house, and I waved as I hurried by.

"Slow down," I could almost hear Ed saying as I opened the back door and started to run up the first flight of stairs. Slowing down had never been part of our routine, but once I became pregnant, Ed began acting so protective that even the kids in the youth group teased him about it.

I tiptoed up the second set of stairs and peered quietly around the door of my husband's office—the youth group gathering room. Ed sat sprawled out on the burgundy couch by the wall, his legs stretched out in front of him. His head was tilted to one side, resting on the back of the couch, his eyes closed. I assumed he had fallen asleep while praying, as I had done earlier that morning.

It had been late the night before when he got home from the men's softball game, and I was glad he could take a few minutes during his lunch break to rest. And this way, I thought, I could sneak up and surprise him. Quietly setting our lunch bag on his desk, I walked toward him.

When I whispered his name, he didn't move.

Kneeling in front of him, I called his name again, louder, touching his cheek. "Ed! Wake up!" I shook his shoulders, slid my hands down his limp arms, and grasped his fingers in my own. They were cold.

My heart pounding, I ran into the hall and down the stairs. I threw open the door of the main office. "Call the ambulance!" I shouted to the secretary. "Something's wrong with Ed! And call Pastor Tim."

Maybe, I told myself as I raced back upstairs, maybe he was so exhausted he couldn't hear me. Maybe he'll be stretching and looking around—maybe I'm overreacting . . . .

But the second I stepped back in the room I could see he hadn't moved. I put my hand on his chest and my ear to his mouth, desperately hoping to feel something.

Nothing.

Throwing my arms around Ed's shoulders I pulled, struggling against his unyielding weight. His head fell forward onto my shoulder. *"Please, Ed,"* I thought as his hair brushed against my cheek. *"Please come back to me."*

"The rescue squad's on the way!" Tim called from the hall as he rushed into the room. "We've got to start CPR," he said, helping to pull Ed until he was flat on the floor. Immediately placing his hands on Ed's chest, Tim began compressions, punctuating each one by crying out for his friend. "God, this is your servant!" he pleaded. "Let him live. Please let him live."

I knelt by my husband's head, placed my lips over his, and began to breathe for him.

As the minutes ticked away with no response, I wanted to scream, *I can't do this any longer!*

The words "It's not about what you *feel*," flashed through my mind—echoing my college drama director's response to the panic of stage fright, "it's *doing* what you've got to do." Without missing a beat, Tim continued chest compressions, and I wiped away the tears that kept falling on my husband's face and breathed for him. All the while pounding on the floor with my fist.

From far away my mind registered the siren of an ambulance, and moments later two paramedics rushed up the stairs and into the office. They took over, one beginning cardiac and respiratory assessment as the other set up support equipment. I stumbled downstairs and into the empty sanctuary where I fell on my knees in front of the first pew.

"You can't take him away from me, God!" I begged out loud. "I love him. I need him more than you do. *You gave us to each other!*"

Tim found me there. "Nadine," he whispered, "the squad is transporting Ed to the ambulance now. Sandy's here with the car. We'll take you to the hospital."

Ed's mother and sister were already at Port Huron's Mercy Hospital emergency room when we rushed in. "We got here just as the ambulance came," my mother-in-law said. "We were standing here when they carried Ed in on the stretcher."

"Have they told you anything?" I asked, afraid to hear what she might say.

"No. Just that the doctor will come out as soon as possible."

A nurse took us to a private waiting area where Ed's brother, Jack, joined us moments later. The nurse recorded our names, and hearing that Tim was Ed's pastor, asked him to come with her. The two of them disappeared through the door into the hallway beyond.

While Jack prayed out loud for his brother, I paced the room, feeling I might explode if I stood still. I tried to pray myself but couldn't get past "Please, God. Please—" Every Scripture verse I could think of turned into "don't trust your own understanding" and then blended into words we had sung at the end of school chapel countless times. "Christ is all I need." *I always thought I believed that, God*—I argued mentally. *But I need Ed too.*

The door opened and Tim came into the waiting room, accompanied by a doctor. As they walked toward us, I wanted time to freeze. I didn't want the doctor to motion us to sit down with him, but he did. I didn't want him to look at each of us for a moment, clear his throat, and say words that would change us forever. But he did.

Ed had experienced cardiac arrest, we were told. They had done all they could. The doctor asked if we wanted to come and see Ed, and still without speaking, we stood and followed as he led us through the door into the hall and stopped outside a patient room. Ed's room. Tim turned and asked if I would be all right; I nodded and followed the others.

I couldn't look at my husband yet. I leaned against the wall just inside the door. One by one Barbara, Gwen, and Jack said goodbye, hugged me, and slipped out of the room. Alone, I turned and walked toward the motionless body lying peacefully in the white hospital bed.

It's too soon, Ed. I miss you already.

Feelings I struggled to suppress since the first moment I held his cold hands now tumbled out. I clutched the bars at the side of the bed, clenching my teeth as tears streamed down my checks. A song from our wedding shot through my mind. "I will be there, you can lean on my shoulder." And now that I desperately needed to lean on that shoulder . . . .

It's too soon for you to go, Ed, I thought. *You promised we'd grow old together. You promised,* I pleaded silently, and then caught myself, thinking of Ed's words when he proposed. "I'll love you faithfully," he had said as he knelt in front of me "and put your needs before my own, as long as I . . . ."

The word hung in air between us. My husband, the love of my life, had kept his promise, for as long as he lived. And now, at the age of twenty-six, he was dead.

I reached out my hand, letting my fingers touch his dark brown hair as it waved over his forehead. "I love you, Ed Hennesey," I said. "I wish I could say those words one more time and know you could hear me."

The minute hand on the clock clicked and I looked up. It was three o'clock. As desperately as I wanted to erase the nightmare of the last two hours, I could not.

I kissed Ed's cheek, turned, and walked out of the room.

At the end of the hall I found a phone and dialed my folks' number. "Dad," I began when my father answered. The next words were the hardest I'd ever spoken. "Ed's gone. He's dead."

I remember collapsing into a chair when we arrived at my mother-in-law's house later that afternoon, covering my face with my hands.

That's when I felt it for the first time. I sat up, and felt it again.

"Oh, Ed," I whispered. "It's the baby. Our baby just moved."

5

WHEN YOU DON'T SEE HIS PLAN

"Shipwrecked on God, stranded on omnipotence."
—Vance Havner

On June 9, 1990, I sat in the front pew of First Baptist Church in Goodells, Michigan, and my family slipped in beside me. The organist began playing "Holy, Holy, Holy," and I tried to make sense of it all.

On June 9, 1987, Ed and I had gone out for our second date, riding bikes and talking about what mattered to us in life. *Three years was not enough time to love him,* I thought. Ed and I had married, and we were getting ready to celebrate our first wedding anniversary. But three days ago I knelt in front of this same pew pleading for my husband's life. And since then, we planned a funeral.

"Wouldn't you like to sit down?" kind people had asked at the funeral home the day before as they came to say goodbye to Ed. My family and most of my friends knew I was pregnant, and I felt their loving support. But as I fought panic and overwhelming confusion moment by moment, I coped the only way I knew how—by trying to be strong and not giving in to my emotions.

"No," I answered. "No, thank you." If I could stand, without leaning, without letting my head rest for more than a moment on the shoulder of a friend, I forced myself to think, maybe I could manage to not fall apart in front of everyone.

As the organist continued playing, I noticed that the church looked the same as it did last Sunday when Ed and I sat across the aisle with the young people. Except for all the flowers in the front.

And the casket.

As the organist began "Great Is Thy Faithfulness," I concentrated on the memorial folder in my lap, desperately trying to disappear into an anonymous place where I could treasure every word of the tribute to my husband. When the organ stopped, Pastor Tim Collard walked to the pulpit.

"Edson F. Hennesey died Wednesday, June 6, at the age of twenty-six," he began. And then he shared what it had been like to be Ed's friend. As I listened I fell in love all over again with the man who had come into my life for such a short time but who was now in God's presence for eternity.

Wayne Hart, my family's pastor from Ohio led in prayer. Pastor Alberto Beltran, Ed's mentor and pastor from our church in Florida, the Primera Iglesia Bautista Hispana, read the Scripture.

The organ music started again. Before the words of the song even began, I knew what they would be. In that moment, the tenuous peace I had felt for the first time in three days disintegrated. This song, I had thought as I numbly wrote out suggestions for the service, had seemed perfect, because Ed and I had sung it last Sunday as a duet during morning worship. "Take my life," it began. "I lay it at the altar." Now the words seemed a mockery. We had sung them wholeheartedly then, but now I knew what they meant and felt as though I had been slapped.

It got worse. The congregation rose for the hymn, "Until Then."

"A heartache here is but a stepping stone," I heard voices around me singing.

I didn't sing the final song either.

God is too wise to be mistaken
God is too good to be unkind.
So when you don't understand,
When you don't see his plan,
When you can't trace His hand,
Trust His heart.

The service ended. I closed the memorial program, smoothed it with my hand, and stood up. As I quietly followed my family down the side aisle of the church, it was all I could do not to smash every stained glass window we passed.

After a long day, I stood at the foot of the stairs in my mother-in-law's home, where I had stayed since leaving the hospital. Ed's mom had opened her home to my family too, and after the graveside service and meal prepared by friends, we all went back there together. I longed to go home to the little apartment Ed and I had shared, but I knew that my family was trying to cushion me against the grief of being there without him. That time would come next week. For now, I shared a few more moments with Barbara, Gwen, and Jack, hugged my mom and dad, and went to the room where I had stayed the last three nights.

My sister, Cindy, had asked if she could stay there with me. I knew she didn't want me to be alone, and as unaccustomed as I was to this kind of attention from my siblings—it would be far more natural to be joking or jostling each other on the basketball court—I knew she wouldn't ask me to talk about my feelings unless I broached the subject.

"I haven't said it yet," I said as I hung up my dress. "But thanks. Thanks for staying with me here tonight."

"I can't say I know how you feel, Nadine," Cindy responded quietly. "But if I could do anything—anything to take away the hurt and carry it myself, I would do it for you."

"I know you would, Cindy," I said turning around. "Thank you. I know you mean that."

I sat next to her on the bed. "It would be easier if we *could* do something, wouldn't it? Or if it made sense."

When Cindy went into the bathroom, I glanced at the bed-side table where Gwen had placed my Bible and other personal belongings she brought from the little home Ed and I had shared. I picked up my journal for a moment. I hadn't written in it for the last three days and didn't think I could now. Then I recognized the small notebook at the bottom of the stack, opened it, and turned to the last page. "Thank You, Lord, for the baby," Ed had begun on the last day he had written in his journal. Slipping into bed, I picked up the pen next to the books. I wasn't sure what I would write, but I wanted the entries in Ed's journal to go on.

"June 9," I began. "Today I buried my husband. I simply wanted to be Ed's wife. Now I'm lost . . . . I am so privileged to carry on Ed's name. I am also humbled. He was a hero of faith, a godly man."

The words we had sung at the end of Ed's funeral played again in my mind. "When you don't see His plan, when you can't trace His hand, trust His heart." *I don't see anything that looks like a plan right now,* I thought, closing the journal and leaning back against the pillow. I slid down beneath the covers, instinctively reached over to the other side of the bed—then turned back and closed my eyes, trying to ignore the fluttering inside my belly.

Prayer changed for me after Ed died. Like a child suddenly thrown into water over her head, I came up desperately for air, pleaded for help, and then sank again.

"I woke up this morning feeling cheated," I wrote five days after the funeral, in words that poured out on paper—prayers I couldn't express any other way. "The reality of his death is beginning to seep into the deep caverns in my heart. I feel like a weight is slowly crushing my chest, and I can't breathe. Never have I loved any person as much as I loved, and still love, Ed. I know in my head that he's with You. But what am I to do without him?"

"Dear God," I wrote later. "I never asked You to give me a beautiful house, nice furniture, or other things. I never even asked You for Ed. But when You did give him to me I knew I had been right in not wanting those other things, because I had the best gift. I loved him, and You took him away. Lord, I feel like You were a potter, forming Ed for Your use. He was wholeheartedly committed to You. But suddenly, You purposefully smashed what was in Your hands. All that's left are the broken pieces. I think You must hate me, God! It's as if seeing all my dreams come true was just a joke. A cruel joke. I hate this. You may be laughing. I'm not."

Confused and lonely, I struggled with the mess of sorting faith from feelings. All of the love and respect I had expressed to God up to that point in life had been sincere. But maybe, I thought, maybe that was because I had always felt secure, like a child on her father's lap. Now it felt like being the kid no one liked, locked out of the house or grounded for life—or both— and not knowing why. I still believed that God's ways were above mine, that He was bigger than all my desires, and that He was not at my beck and call. But I found myself expressing thoughts that had never occurred to me before. Had I been naïve about God's nature? Sheltered from reality? I knew God was big enough to handle my honesty. But does He *care* about how we feel?

"People say You are a God of love and are gracious," I wrote in my journal one night. "I feel like those two aspects have been taken from my life. Today when I flipped the radio on I heard Warren Wiersbe say, 'We don't live by explanations. We live by promises.' I know in my head that You do not break Your promises, but my heart points out a few that appear to have been broken. The past week I have struggled, and part of that struggle has been my anger with You. Lord, I don't know what You are doing."

On our first anniversary I drove past the Thomas Edison Inn, a restaurant that overlooks the St. Clair River in Port Huron. That's where we would have been having dinner that night. I knew this from overhearing Ed's call for reservations just before he died. I missed everything about my husband—his loving affection from the moment we woke up together, his sense of humor that helped keep life in perspective, his concern for others, and his vision for our life together. I missed him.

"Why did You take him away so suddenly? If Ed was going to spend eternity with You, why couldn't You have left him here longer?" I wrote. "What is supposed to be an exciting, joyful time in our lives has turned into my nightmare."

Three days later was my birthday.

"The best birthday I will ever have will be last year's when we were together on our honeymoon," I wrote that night. "This birthday I am lost. My life is empty, Lord. It is going to be Your grace if I survive this. I don't want another birthday. I want to go home."

As my pregnancy became increasingly obvious, relating to others in day-to-day encounters took on an awkward complexity. Maybe people thought "Congratulations" would sound flippant so soon after Ed died, or maybe "I'm sorry" would come across as too negative in light of a baby's arrival. One thing I heard a lot was that God must know how strong I am and knows I could handle this. I would usually nod, mentally preferring to be weak and have Ed.

One Sunday evening after the church service a well-meaning lady expressed her attempt at giving me comfort. "I am so sorry about what happened to Ed," she began. "It's a good thing you're so young because it will be easy for you to find someone else."

I bit my lip and looked away, trying to keep from saying something I would regret later. *I don't want another one. I love the one I had,* I thought as I turned and walked out.

A month had gone by since the funeral, and I still couldn't bring myself to open my Bible. But one day, tentatively, I opened Ed's. Inside I discovered an envelope, with my name on it. Slowly I opened it and found a card—for no particular reason other than the words Ed had written. "I love you, Nadine," it said. "You are precious to me." The card was dated June 6. My mind played back the details of that morning, how he had fussed over me, encouraging me to sleep in while he went into the kitchen to make his breakfast and have devotions. "A note on the day he died . . . it's not a coincidence," I wrote that night. "You had him write then, didn't You, Lord?"

Through the summer months, I tried to move forward. I lived with my sister-in-law Gwen and her family, trying to hang on to threads of what life was all about. Sitting alone in the bleachers of the softball field early one morning, I remembered watching Ed play there. That night I went to the church team's game and was touched to see that all the guys had the number 11, Ed's number, written on their shirts.

My brother and sister, Sheri and Troy, came up to go along with me on the youth group's bike ride and camping trip—the activity Ed had been working on the day he died. My mom and dad came up for a weekend in August to help me tie up loose ends because I was preparing to move back to Ohio. My brother David came with them and asked if he could stay with me until it was time to move three weeks later.

Since David was born when I was in high school, during my college years I had saved Saturdays as often as possible to play with him. We would pack a lunch and go on exciting expeditions—planned to keep David in suspense because I never told him what we were going to do or where we were going. But I knew being with me now was no fun at all for him. I found myself apologizing again and again. "I just don't feel like myself."

"It's okay," my brother would say each time.

In September, I packed the last of my life as a wife into boxes, and my dad, mom, David, and I drove to Ohio. My folks had encouraged me to come home for the baby's birth and stay as long as I wanted to stay afterwards. By moving their washer and dryer into the basement, they were able to transform the laundry room into a private living space for the baby and me.

Who am I now? I often thought as I puttered about, trying to be useful around the house. *I lived here once as a daughter, now I'm a wife without a husband, about to become a mother. And what will I do to support a baby?* "I know I am in no position to put conditions on You," I wrote in my prayer journal. "But Father, please call me to a ministry I could not have done while I was married . . . something unique to my situation."

One day as I was unpacking the boxes I brought from Michigan, I found a journal I had forgotten about tucked in the bottom. In a letter to God written at the end of my junior year at Cedarville I wrote, "This life is rough and short. Living for You is rough, but it will surpass the heartaches I would have if I didn't live for You." I closed with this request, "Never let me marry an individual until my commitment to You is one of which You are proud."

In an entry written during my senior year at school, I wrote, "In a basketball game, a player feels a lot of pressure from the fans. It's easy to get caught up in what they want you to do. To be honest, it's not too hard to please them because they look for the outward show. But You, Lord, look for both the outward and the inward performance. I don't want You to ever have to set me on the bench because I'm messing up the play of the game."

Stuffing the journal in the bottom drawer of my dresser didn't keep me from thinking about it. Living out your faith sure is a lot harder than making A's in Bible class, I thought. "Lord, I'm tired of this test," I wrote later. "I want it to be over. Give me an F, but give me my husband. I will admit that my love for You has not grown since Ed died. Right now I am just a weak, clay vessel. You've set before me a race, I know, but I keep looking in the other lane and want to trade."

Maybe, I forced myself to admit . . . the problem was me. I was trying to see God's plan, but maybe I just wasn't in it anymore. Maybe I had been benched.

6

BABY STEPS

"Be assured that Ed is not only well cared for and content . . .
but knows perfect joy. Very likely he prays for you.
I think God must share with our husbands the victories and
joys in our lives. Surely Ed knows about your baby."
—Elisabeth Elliot Gren, personal letter

"If it's a boy . . . "

I thought back to the night Ed and I had lain in bed before going to sleep, ticking off possible names for the baby. "If it's a boy," Ed said, "I think we should name him Josiah."

"And if it's a girl?" I asked. He turned his head on the pillow and looked at me, and then we both said it at the same time. "Lydia."

As my clothes got tighter every day, so did the panic about my new life around the corner. *Being a single mother was something that happened to someone else,* I had always thought. The scenario was entirely different now, though. I wasn't looking in from the outside, making suggestions from a secure, stable life somewhere else. I was the one saying to myself, "This isn't what I had in mind, and I don't really like how it feels."

I recalled that as a college student I sat in church behind young couples as they held their little ones on their laps, and I took for granted that my married life would be picture perfect—just like theirs. In moments when I couldn't help myself, I would visualize Ed in the photograph of our family as I always imagined we would be–laughing and having fun together. Then I would see the picture again with an empty space where Ed had been.

In those moments my greatest fear was that our child's life would always be shadowed by my sadness. For someone who grew up with a reputation for her sense of fun, it seemed surreal that I couldn't remember the last time I had laughed. As inadequate as I felt, I longed to be a good mother to the little one I carried kicking and turning inside me. This baby would be my living connection to the man whose life—despite letters tucked safely away and our wedding photo in its special place—was now a memory.

When I went for my maternity check-up with Dr. Filomeno Flores on November 1, he said it was time for the baby to make an appearance and that I should check into Greene Memorial Hospital in Xenia to be induced the next morning. That night, in the quiet of my room, I journaled about the day to come, and for a moment I allowed myself to imagine the joy on Ed's face as the doctor placed our son or daughter in his arms. Then, pulling up against my lonely reality, I closed my journal, thinking about the date I had just written.

Sixteen months earlier—to the day—I became a bride.

Less than a year later, I became a widow.

And tomorrow I would become a mother.

I looked around at the room with the bassinet against the wall close to my bed and the cradle pulled close to the rocker my mother had sat in to hold all of us. My baby would be on schedule. The room was ready, and whether I was prepared for this or not didn't make any difference. From tomorrow onward, I would be a mother.

The next day my family came to the hospital to be with me and help me through a long day of labor. Sometime in the afternoon, Ed's brother, Jack, arrived from Michigan, saying that his mother and sister would be coming by as soon as the baby got here. As the night wore on, it looked like the baby might not come until the next day, and I longed for labor to end.

However, at 11:06 p.m. on November 2, 1990, the waiting was over. Dr. Flores announced, "Congratulations! It's a girl!"

From what seemed like a long way away I heard the baby cry once, and then Dr. Flores told us she was healthy.

A girl. I knew her name, but I couldn't say it out loud yet.

"Would you like to hold her, Nadine?" I heard the nurse say. Unprepared for any emotional response, I held out my arms, and the nurse gently placed in them a soft, pink bundle.

She's so tiny, I thought. The little person I was holding felt like a doll . . . soft, tiny, and beautiful, but not quite real. "Hello," I whispered. She turned her head, covered in a knit cap, and opened her eyes. I caught my breath as she blinked once and then held my gaze. Many babies have blue eyes at birth, I knew, and the color sometimes changes. But as I looked into this tiny baby's bright blue eyes I saw immediately how like Ed's they were.

"Hello, Lydia," I said. "You've got your daddy's eyes, don't you?" She blinked again and then smiled. In that moment, my heart was completely captured, and I knew I would love her forever.

In the quiet of my room, after Lydia was taken to the nursery, I tried to sleep but couldn't. "I can just hear Ed running up and down the streets of heaven telling everyone, 'I have a baby girl!' " I wrote in my journal. "And in that one moment, when Lydia smiled at me, something clicked. It's like I'm hearing a voice from a great distance, saying 'You're back in the game in a different position: *Mom.*'"

The next morning I woke up, eager to see Lydia. I could hear the nurses in the hall talking as they took other babies to their mothers. Finally, a nurse pushed a bassinet into the room. "I'm sorry she's so late," she said. "Your baby's been entertaining all of us down in the nursery, laughing and smiling."

"Is that unusual?" I asked.

"Oh, yes," she replied. "Usually the babies are so sleepy they just lie there. But this one's been awake and happy all morning."

That night when my nurses offered to take Lydia back to the nursery so I could sleep through the night, I shook my head. "No thanks. I'd like her to stay here."

This is my baby, and from now on she stays with me, I thought as I reached over from my bed to rest my hand on her bassinet. If she cried I would pick her up. And I couldn't wait to hear her laugh again.

For the first ten months of Lydia's life, we lived with my family. During the day I cared for my daughter out in the main part of the house. Since I had grown up in this house with a playpen in the living room and a high chair in the kitchen, it seemed natural seeing a baby there getting hugs and kisses from my family as they passed through the house. David, who was just eight years old and seemed more like a big brother, loved telling Lydia that he was her uncle. "Just wait until you're bigger," he would say, "and I'll teach you to play baseball."

After supper each night, I went into the room that was our own little home and rocked my baby, telling her stories about her daddy and singing along with the gentle, recorded lullabies that calmed me while I held her. "Sleep sound in Jesus," I would sing with Michael Card. "Sweetheart of my heart . . . the dark of night will not keep us apart. When I lay you down in your bed for the night, He holds you gently 'til morning is light."

It was hard to picture myself without her. "I think that if I hadn't had Lydia," I wrote in the prayer journal I began after Ed died, "I would have become a workaholic and just dived into activity twenty-four hours a day. I would never have dealt with what happened . . . just wiped it away and locked the door of my heart. But with Lydia I have time to think."

One day as I read again the journal Ed kept in college, I came to the entry he began by quoting Jim Elliot: "He is no fool to give what he cannot keep to gain what he cannot lose." Jim and his friends had given their lives to take the gospel to the Auca Indians in Ecuador, and as Ed reflected on their story, he asked God to use *his* life too, "no matter how long or short it might be." The courage lived out by Jim and his friends—Nate Saint, Roger Youderian, Pete Fleming, and Ed McCully—had inspired me as well. But that day as I read, my thoughts turned to their wives, who forgave their husbands' murderers and asked for help in carrying on their husbands' vision. They had lived through the worst day of their lives, and with God's grace they had seen good come from it. Although I didn't compare the circumstances of my situation to theirs, I felt overcome by my inability to live in a way that could possibly bring good from my own husband's death. Not really expecting anything in return, I poured out my heart in a letter to Jim's widow Elisabeth Elliot Gren, expressing my heartfelt admiration.

The gracious letter Elisabeth sent back was a tremendous comfort. "Be assured that Ed is not only well cared for and content," she began, "but knows perfect joy. Very likely he prays for you. I think God must share with our husbands the victories and joys in our lives. Surely Ed knows about your baby."

As much as I longed for Ed to be with us, I knew he had finished the course God set before him. But I hadn't. Ed had prayed for Lydia from the moment he knew I was pregnant, he had helped to name her, and I was certain that he would have been a wonderful father. I longed for him to hold his child. With an ache in my heart, I asked God to love her in a special way. I had always believed in God as a "heavenly Father." Could He be all Lydia needed as a father now and as she grew up? Was God sufficient to care for both of us?

When Lydia was ten months old, she took her first steps alone. The time had come, I felt, for us to establish our own home, and I accepted a teaching job in Michigan, close to where Ed and I had lived. I treasured the way Lydia had been part of my family for her first months of life and hoped that now she would have a chance to get to know her daddy's family too.

Packing our lives once again into cardboard boxes loaded in the back of my car, I put my daughter into her car seat and hugged my family. "Thanks for loving me through the hardest days of my life," I told my mom and dad as we stood in the driveway.

While living in Michigan, one weekend I went to visit Ed's Uncle Les and Aunt Corinne, who worshiped at a church in Grand Ledge. Their young pastor, Eric Mounts, was someone I had known in Ohio. Our family had been great fans of Eric during his days as a college basketball star at Cedarville, and when I was in high school, he had come to our church as an intern. It seemed providential that his message that Sunday was about the widow's persistent knocking on the door of prayer, as told in Luke 18. "Her supplication wasn't hit or miss," Eric said, "not just at the time of crisis." He added that there are times in life when we can't stay where it's safe and secure, and in those times, the living God knows and cares about our need. Although the widow was easy prey for mistreatment, her case was just. In an upside-down world, she was right. Unlike the unjust judge, God seeks our persevering prayer, and He will respond—even if we can't see that now. "Move forward," Eric encouraged us as we listened. "Move forward, chin up, knees down."

I knew Eric's words weren't planned for me—he didn't even know I would be there that day. But they could have been. Although I would miss my husband the rest of my life, in the year after his death, I had given God the pain and asked Him to use me—as I was. To "move forward," as I had just heard in Eric's providential encouragement.

Lydia was taking baby steps. Though with admittedly child-like faith on my part, so, it seemed, was I.

While we got settled in Michigan, my brother-in-law unexpectedly provided us with a house he owned, rent-free—asking only that I take care of maintenance and utility bills.

Ed's sister, Gwen, became a great friend. She had been only nine years old when their father had died, and she had grown up very close to Ed. Neither of us tried to tell the other that we should be over our grief by now; we just went through it side-by-side, spending a lot of time together.

As Lydia grew during the next three years, I worked to support her with a combination of part-time teaching, coaching, and selling kitchen tools for Pampered Chef. Being a mother completely changed my perspective on the importance of faithfulness. I had always thought about how I would be careful in the big decisions and responsibilities of life. But the responsibility God brought into my life was a tiny one—a happy, bouncy little girl.

We went everywhere we could together. When I coached high school volleyball, for instance, Lydia would come along, and although I brought coloring books and other things she could do while sitting on the bleachers, she preferred to run around and help chase the balls.

That summer, when Lydia was four, I started making plans for her to go to kindergarten. I was ready to apply for a full-time teaching position again, but a thought in the back of my mind kept surfacing. Why did I need to teach in the United States? And why had God given Ed such a burden for Peru?

I had to find out.

7

MUD, SWEAT, AND TEARS

*"One truth about missionaries is that they are not glorious,
super-spiritual, super-human people. They laugh, they cry.
They misunderstand. They understand. They work. They sweat."*
—Nadine Hennesey, after one year in Peru

"Mommy, it's just like a roller coaster," Lydia whispered, her eyes open wide. The comparison was a good one, I thought, knowing that she was thinking about her going-away trip to the amusement park the day before. As our small plane suddenly lost altitude, labored to climb, and dropped again, I nodded and plastered a smile on my face.

Oh, the faith of a child. Lydia was right about the roller coaster—except I was thinking about the roller coaster of our life. As we flew out of the Dayton International Airport that morning, Lydia and I were starting a new chapter, and I was sure we were on our way to a life-changing, transforming experience. Hours later, in Miami, as we transferred from the smaller regional airliner to a 747 and headed out in the night sky to Peru, it seemed that our spiritual journey so far had been a long, bumpy ride.

A few months earlier, as I pulled letters and bills from my mailbox, I glanced at the cover of a publication from the Association of Baptists for World Evangelism (ABWE). I noticed the words "Wanted—*Teachers*." Turning to the article and scanning the locations requested for short-term teachers, I saw it—there at the bottom of the list was *Peru*. Still standing by the mailbox, I made a decision. Before I could lose heart, I walked into the house and called the number listed inside the magazine. Would ABWE be interested in a single mother with her four-year-old daughter, I asked Barb, the woman who answered the phone?

"Yes," she answered without hesitation. "Would you like me to send an application?"

"Yes," I answered just as quickly.

When the ABWE representative responded to my application, she told me that a missionary couple in Iquitos, Peru, had requested a first-grade teacher for their daughter, Natasha. *I could teach the girls together,* I thought. That night I showed Lydia a map of Peru. "How would you like to go to school here?" I asked.

And now we were on our way—gliding through the air toward our home for the next twelve months. My concern about not knowing anyone in Peru was put to rest, ironically, as the couple sitting next to us on the plane introduced themselves. "Chuck and Carrie Porter," the gentleman said, and I soon discovered that they were part of the same ministry team we were going to work with in the jungle city of Iquitos, the capital city of Peru's Maynas Province, in the northern Leroto Region of the country. The Porters told us that they had a grown daughter, Lynn, who was still serving there.

When we landed in Iquitos at 11:30 that night, I nudged Lydia, who had fallen asleep. "Wake up, honey," I said. "We're here!" Excited, she stretched, unbuckled her seatbelt, grabbed her stuffed rabbit Puffy, and jumped out ahead of me into the aisle.

I fumbled toward her, my arms full of carry-on luggage, and caught up just as she reached the open exit door.

When we walked off the plane and into the humid night air, we saw Peruvians, some in grass skirts and some with painted faces, dancing in a circle on the tarmac, holding torches that flamed against the night sky. "Really cool," I started to say, and then I looked down at my four-year-old, frozen in her tracks. From behind me, Mr. Porter asked if he could help, and as he picked Lydia up, she buried her head in his shoulder, pointing at the dancers. He whispered something to her, and she relaxed and giggled. "Don't worry, Mom," she said reassuringly as she looked back at me. "They're supposed to do that. They're the welcoming committee!"

After we made our way into the terminal, my luggage was thrown onto a counter, and the inspector demanded I open every piece. As I watched him go through each suitcase, I panicked—suddenly realizing that I had left the key to the largest bag in a purse back home. Just as he was ready to pull that bag up to the inspection table, a higher-ranking man said something to him in Spanish and waved us through. I breathed a sigh of relief. "Perfect timing, Lord."

After going through customs, we stepped outside and were greeted by the ABWE welcoming committee that had come to the airport just for us. A young man standing by a jeep waved and ran over. "Rich Donaldson," he said, holding out his hand to me. "My wife, Beth, is home with Natasha," he said, turning toward Lydia. "She's asleep but can't wait to meet you tomorrow." He introduced the rest who were able to come, and they quickly loaded our luggage onto Rich's jeep. We took off, zipping among vehicles on amazingly busy streets until we arrived at the Donaldson's house, where Lydia and I spent our first night in Peru's Amazon rain forest.

The next morning Natasha and her brother, Nate, sat with Lydia—laughing and talking while Beth served us breakfast. I thought about the last twenty-four hours. We had been officially welcomed, had met new friends, and had my locked suitcase opened by Rich, who was able to open it by breaking the lock (so now Lydia and I had clothes to wear). I was reminded rather quickly that I was not in charge of much at all.

Before our school schedule kicked in, some of the ministry team welcomed us to join them in different parts of the city outreach. Our neighbor, Lynn Porter, took us next door where she had begun a ministry for the deaf. Watching Lynn connect enthusiastically through sign language was exciting—even more so because, as her folks had told me as we talked on the plane, she had experienced an injury at birth that significantly reduced the mobility of her left hand.

Another neighbor in our compound was Darlene Hull, who had been with the team for more than 20 years. From the very start, this "Michigan-born Peruvian," helped me navigate my new cultural landscape.

"The kids can't come to us," Darlene explained one night as she packed up for a children's outreach on the Amazon River. "So we go to them. Would you and Lydia like to join me?" I agreed right away, thinking of all the times when, as a high school student, I picked up neighborhood kids for activities in our church. This would be just like that—except for the part about the rain forest and the Amazon River. We weren't in Ohio anymore, that was for sure.

The next evening, with a day's worth of food in our possession, we jumped onto a launch that transported people along the Amazon, just like a bus on water. Joining us was a young Peruvian girl named Julie, who helped with the children's ministry. Friendly shoppers on their way to and from stops along the river crowded around to greet us. They were especially interested in sandy-haired, blue-eyed Lydia, who was the youngest one on the launch. She quickly became the main attraction. We slept on a hammock; the bathroom was a hole in the back of the boat. The trip ended up taking two days and two nights. When we arrived at our destination, the American family hosting us hurried to the river to greet us and then ran to tell the village children that we were there. It was a great first lesson in flexibility—daily vacation Bible school, Peruvian style.

More than one week after setting out on our Amazon adventure, we arrived back at our apartment in Iquitos. It was time to set up my classroom for the first lesson of the new school year.

The days and weeks fell into a familiar routine of school lessons during the day and helping with special projects on weekends. I loved getting out among the Peruvian people, and I began to feel at home shopping in the local markets. To travel, we would go out and wave down a moto taxi—a little cart that was like a motorcycle-tricycle with a canopy over the top. These noisy little transports were everywhere—and for less than a US dollar we could ride all over Iquitos.

My Spanish was getting better—although I still got myself into trouble on the fine points.

I would go to the meat shop and do my best to communicate. "Carne," I'd say in Spanish (*meat* in English), and then I would make the sound of the animal meat I wanted. Like "moo" for beef. Or I would act out some trait of the animal. That's how I learned—once they told me the word for "beef" or "chicken," I had it. And it really didn't bother me that everyone was laughing as we walked out of the shop.

One morning Lydia and I went to the bakery to get eight bread rolls. "Ochenta, por favor," I said proudly, pointing into the basket of rolls. The baker looked at me, nodded, and went into the back of the shop. We waited a long, *long* time, and when the baker came back he had *eighty* rolls. I paid him, and Lydia and I walked out, loaded down with enough daily bread for weeks.

"Why didn't you tell him you meant *'ocho,'* Mom?" Lydia asked as soon as we stepped outside.

"He went to a lot of trouble," I told her, "and spent a lot of time. I'm just glad I had enough money."

"But, Mom, what are we going to do with eighty rolls?"

"What do you think we should do?"

Lydia thought for a moment. "We could give them away. The kids here are always hungry."

By the time we got home, we had eight rolls left. And some new friends.

One day I met a new family who had just joined the full-time ministry team in Peru. They came by the apartment building, and when I opened the door, standing there was an athletic-looking young man and his wife, carrying their little son and two white poodles. "Jim, Roni, and Cory Bowers," they said, introducing themselves.

Roni and I became friends, and later, when the Bowers needed a place to live while working on plans for a houseboat, I invited them to stay with us. Roni told me how she and Jim had met at Piedmont Baptist College in Winston-Salem, North Carolina, and discovered their mutual passion for missions. Their goal now was to share the gospel and humanitarian aid by living on a houseboat that would let them connect regularly with people in villages beyond the city and mountains. Roni's energy and sense of humor were contagious.

Intrigued by the idea of working from a houseboat, I asked the Donaldsons more about that one night as we talked over dinner. They explained that families would often take extended trips, stopping at villages along the Amazon, and staying, as needed, to help with medical needs, construction work, and education. One such family was in the final stage of their trip, they said, due back in Iquitos in about a week. This would be the perfect opportunity to see some of this outreach, Rich suggested. He called his brother, Kevin, a pilot, who agreed to transport us to where the houseboat was docked.

From our viewpoint above the wings of Kevin's small white plane, we watched the Amazon River twist along stretches of lush green jungle dotted by villages along the shore. Miles later, Kevin spotted the docked houseboat we were to meet. He radioed down to the owner, Andy Large, and landed on the river nearby. Andy and his wife, Diane, Americans who were both born and raised in Peru, and their daughter, Susie, were there waiting for us.

What had been visible from the plane as green treetops and huts here and there came into closer focus as we started the trip back toward Iquitos by boat. Andy and Diane had already begun village "house churches," as we might think of them, in the places where we stopped on the last part of the trip. Each time we pulled onshore, people ran out of the jungle, and, recognizing their friends, shouted greetings. Andy would play a few notes on his trumpet as an invitation to join for a meeting, and about fifteen minutes later we would gather in a nearby shelter or clearing. Men sat on one side of the circle, women and children on the other, all huddled close together. As Andy taught from the Bible, I tried to follow his fluent Spanish by translating mentally, but at the inevitable point when it went over my head, I would lean back and take in the fascinating scene. Surrounded by the lush green foliage and beautiful flowers of the rain forest, I watched the villagers, smiling, nodding, and sometimes singing in spontaneous response. As I looked over at Lydia, sitting in a group of children with her new friend, Susie, I hoped she would always remember this uninhibited community worship deep in a jungle of Peru.

"It was a great trip," I wrote in a note to my parents about our houseboat adventure. "Not the normal 'jump in your car and run here and there' kind of thing." The one thing I didn't tell them until later was that I had contracted dengue fever and had spent much of the time lying on the side of the boat with my head hanging off the edge. I hadn't felt well the day before, but I kept telling myself the nausea I was feeling was probably from being in the sun too much. That evening, as I sat under a grass hut for a Bible study, Susie said that my face was really red and that she could feel the heat radiating from my body.

That night, lying in our berth of the rocking houseboat, I struggled between not wanting to move for fear I would lose everything and wanting to step out for fresh air but feeling so dizzy I was afraid I would fall overboard. The next morning Diane asked how I had slept, and I explained how I had felt but said I was much better now. She took my temperature, and it was 103 degrees. Despite the rocky trip back, it really was a great adventure. Being able to see a family's ongoing ministry to villagers who lived in the jungle had reminded me of Ed's passion to push through traditional boundaries to reach people with the gospel.

A door of cross-cultural connection that was becoming increasingly valuable to me was learning from the nationals. Julie, our young Peruvian helper, quickly became my best friend. Since she didn't let on how awful I must have sounded in Spanish, we had great conversations. One day, after answering some of her questions about my family, I asked her how old she was. She smiled, shrugged, and said she wasn't really sure. "I'm about your age," she said, "and I have many brothers and sisters."

Then she told an incredible story from her past. When she was just a baby, her mother had taken Julie to stay with her oldest sister. While her mother was out shopping, an older woman came by the house and said she couldn't have children but wanted a child. "My sister sold me to her," Julie said. "The woman loved me and raised me as her own. It wasn't until I was much older that I found out I had been adopted."

After hearing her story, I understood better why Julie often volunteered to work at an orphanage downriver. She invited Lydia and me to come with her one Saturday. When we walked into the room of orphaned and abandoned children, I felt an immediate recollection of Amy Carmichael's passion for orphans in India that had inspired me as a young girl. "Love through me, love of God," Amy had written—a heart cry I had understood intellectually then, but now felt. Another hero of mine was George Mueller, whose vision for orphans in England had shaped my idea of life-changing faith. A resolve was already forming in my heart—that if God did guide me to come back to Peru after this year of short-term work, it would be to help children like these.

After that first visit, Julie, Lydia, and I decided to go back to the orphanage one Saturday every month. We brought games, decorations, and a cake, so we could have a party for the children whose birthdays were that month. By now, traveling on short trips up and down the river really did feel like hopping in a bus. We would catch a ride in the morning, settle in with the villagers heading home from the market with their chickens and fresh corn (or whatever—I wasn't always sure), and lean back against the tall sides of the boat as the other passengers ate, played games, and slept. In the afternoon we would catch one of the many boats coming back. No big deal.

But one Saturday, after waiting for a boat returning in the afternoon, Julie suddenly turned to me with a look of unusual alarm. "I just remembered," she said, "it's a holiday tomorrow, so there probably won't be a boat coming back." We discussed our options. We could walk for three hours through the jungle at the edge of the river, but as I looked down at Lydia my mind raced, filling in the frightening details of that scenario. I realized that soon the mosquitoes would swarm in from the river and settle like a black cloud, and although I had learned by then to never go anywhere without repellant, it would be poor defense now.

Just then, a man ran up to us. He knew we needed a ride, he said quickly, and he had a friend with a boat. He ran off, and before long, another man in a tiny boat pulled up and said he had come to help. Even as I thanked God for this quick answer to prayer, I couldn't help noting that this "boat" was unlike any I had ever seen yet. It was about three feet across, and other than its outer ledge, was completely open. The real problem, I could see, was balance—or lack thereof. The man must have read the concern on my face. "I have a flashlight," he called out, smiling. This was important—we weren't going to be back until after dark, and he needed a light to see the shoreline. "Gracias," Julie said, and I nodded. We had no choice.

As we stepped on board, the boat began to rock vigorously. I strapped Lydia into the life jacket I took wherever we went, set her firmly on my lap, and Julie and I took opposite sides of center, sitting on the ledge. Across the bottom of the boat, large grubs crawled around in bowls of what looked like grated carrots, but I planted my feet beside them to keep balance. I locked eyes with Julie, and when the boat tipped her way, I leaned to counterbalance. On her side, Julie did the same. As the rocking subsided slightly, Lydia fell asleep, her head resting against my neck. *Her faith's a lot stronger than mine,* I thought, visualizing the alligators below the water, a situation that could only get worse after dark—flashlight or no flashlight.

With my eyes open every second, I prayed. "Help," I said out loud. "Please, Lord, help us." The sun slipped over the horizon as we glided across the dark, glassy water reflecting shadows in the moonlight.

Waking up as we pulled onshore, Lydia asked, "Did I miss anything?"

"Not a thing, honey," I answered gratefully.

Because Julie had helped in many ministries around Peru, she knew local pastors in the country's capital city of Lima and in the mountain cities of Huaraz, Arequipa, and Cusco. She helped arrange for us to stay with three Peruvian pastors and their families.

After spending some time with them and after being inspired by their perspective on living as Jesus lived, I described their example in my July prayer letter that year. "I would like to share what 'missions' means to me," I began.

"Missions is getting up at midnight to meet three weary travelers. It is giving up your only blanket so your guests will stay warm . . . It's willingly raising a baby that is not your own . . . Shining another's shoes when you have no shoes of your own. Missions is joy in serving Jesus with a love that penetrates the rags and reaches the heart."

One Saturday when we were visiting the pastors, one of them invited us to a service at a church he was starting farther up the mountain. At six o'clock the next morning, we got on a bus, rode for an hour, got off, crossed the bridge over a river, and then started trekking up a muddy pathway. I was carrying Lydia on my back and having trouble keeping up. *This guy's in a lot better physical shape than I am*, I was thinking as I watched the young pastor leading the way. Just then a man leading a small donkey came around the curve of the road. The pastor stopped him, pointed up the mountain as the man nodded, and then picked up Lydia and set her on the donkey. The expression on Lydia's face was clear: It seemed to say, *Finally! Now we are doing this right.* For about forty-five minutes more we walked and she rode, smiling the whole time. One river crossing, one mountain climb, one muddy walk, and one donkey ride later, we arrived, and the pastor enthusiastically greeted his new and growing congregation of two women and eight children.

Coming back down was easier. We took a path that led more directly to the river, but at this crossing, instead of a bridge, there was a pulley system—or what the pastor called a "zip ride."

"You sit on this board," he explained. "Hang onto the ropes and that guy across the river pulls you across. You'll swing this way and then the other," he went on, demonstrating. Julie looked over at me, still standing there.

"Who'll go first?" Julie asked and then grabbed the rope. "Now watch. The only tricky thing is hanging on when the rope breaks." She glanced back at me over her shoulder. "Just kidding."

When it was our turn, Lydia and I got on the board together and inch-by-inch were pulled across the river.

Life in Peru was beginning to feel less like being visitors from America and more like being neighbors. My cousin Rick took a break from his job to come and stay with us over Christmas break, and it was fun to watch Lydia show him around and help him feel at home. "You have to take a siesta" which, she explained, meant having your afternoon nap while sleeping in a swinging hammock. So Rick and Lydia arranged two hammocks, one over the other, and pretended to take siestas—with a lot of laughing, reading books, and throwing toys back and forth mixed in.

Our apartment was at the edge of Iquitos, and as we got to know the kids in our neighborhood, I could see how popular anything to do with sports was to them. Even if I couldn't carry on a deep conversation in Spanish with them, I figured, maybe we could play baseball together. The boys who became our neighborhood "little league" were great at hitting the ball, but then they would run all over the field without following any kind of pattern. And once we started, they wanted to play all the time.

One day as I was leaving the apartment, a group of about twenty boys ran over, ready to play. When I explained that they would have to wait, they stomped off angrily. I came home later to find the flowers in the front yard ripped up and dirt thrown all over the courtyard. Feeling terrible that this happened because of me, I cleaned it up myself. The next day, the same thing happened again. I rounded up the boys, gave them buckets of water and cleaning supplies, and told them to clean up the mess they made. It was a big job, so I was surprised when, not long afterwards, they came over again, trashed the front of the compound, and then knocked on my door.

"Look at the mess we made," they said, smiling. "Can we clean it up?" I looked from one boy to another, puzzled. I didn't know if it was just getting a little attention they wanted, or if, since they didn't have running water in their homes, they made a game of splashing around in the water.

"Look, guys," I said, appealing to their sense of reason. "You can't keep doing this or they're going to kick me out of here." The next time the boys messed up and offered to clean up, I held onto the bucket. "No," I said. "I mean it. This time I'm cleaning up, and you'll have to wait to play ball another day." After that there were no more messes. And before long some of them even caught on to fielding strategies! Pointing back and forth from the bases to me, saying something about "Coach," they would yell instructions to the others and start over.

One day Roni Bowers came by my apartment. "Could you please take care of our two dogs for a few days?" she asked. In order to get some necessary supplies to finish building their houseboat, she explained, they needed to make a quick trip back to the States.

"Sure, " I said, and told Roni not to worry about a thing while she was gone.

The dogs stayed in the enclosed yard during the day, and at night they slept in a little room off the courtyard. On Sunday morning I got up early to pray, but every time I closed my eyes, this voice in my head said, "Go check on the dogs." When I did, I discovered that the enclosure where I put them the night before had been broken into, and the dogs were gone! I ran out into the street and asked the first boy I saw if he had seen the two little poodles. As I was coming back down the street toward my apartment after circling the neighborhood, two of my young baseball players ran to meet me. "We know where the dogs are," they said breathlessly, pointing to a house across the street. "We saw a man carry them over there."

I marched over to the courtyard and opened the gate. The two men inside turned toward me, a surprised look on their faces. And there beside them were Roni's poodles. I walked past them without a word, put one dog under each arm, and walked back to the gate. Before opening it, I turned back to face the men still staring at me. "Gracias," I said, and walked out.

A few minutes later there was a knock at my door. My neighbor Darlene had heard about the rescue by then, and she joined me to see what was going on. She was standing there with me when I answered the knock at the front door. The two men from across the street started talking very fast—both at the same time.

"They say you owe them money," Darlene interpreted, just as quickly. "They say the animals had been roaming the streets and needed to be protected."

"Tell them that these 'animals' couldn't reach up and open the door by themselves," I shot back. Then I turned to the men and speaking as clearly in Spanish as I could, said, "These are our dogs, and you came in here and took them!"

Both men stared at me, turned to each other, argued for a moment, and then walked away, still arguing.

"What did I say?" I asked Darlene, feeling like I had unexpectedly won a wrestling match.

"You said, '*dogs*,'" Darlene replied. "Apparently the plan was to sell the poodles for their beautiful white *wool*, and then for *lamb chops*. It seems the men thought the dogs were *sheep*."

When the Bowers returned, I gratefully returned the poodles and kept the story of their rescue to myself.

The last time Roni and I sat together, we talked about loss—the loss of her child through miscarriage and my loss of a spouse. We talked about the struggles of heart we shared and our confidence in God as our foundation, knowing that somehow, someway, He knew what was best.

I will always treasure our friendship, especially in light of what happened to her less than five years later.

On April 20, 2001, while living in another part of the world, I heard the tragic news. Veronica "Roni" Bowers and her seven-month-old daughter, Charity, were dead. The Bowers were on a trip to pick up a visa for their newly adopted little girl when the small Cessna 185 pontoon plane they were riding—the same plane on which Lydia and I had flown earlier—was mistaken for one carrying drugs. It was sprayed with gunfire. A single bullet penetrated Roni's heart and entered Charity's skull, killing them both. The pilot, Kevin Donaldson, sustained bullet wounds in both legs but miraculously managed to land the plane on the Amazon River. Jim pulled his son Cory from the plane, and then he retrieved the bodies of his wife and daughter. For weeks I could think of nothing else. Roni's perseverance in life can be summarized in the verse, "For to me to live is Christ and to die is gain." Even now, I am challenged to give my all to the very end, as she did.

It wasn't long before that year in South America—one that had stretched ahead of us the previous July—was suddenly over. As Lydia and I boarded the plane in Iquitos to head back to the United States, I thought of the night we arrived. The first question I had then was if I could be a single mom on the mission field. Looking at the tan five-year-old grinning up at me as we settled into our seats, I smiled back and decided to stop worrying.

The other question I needed to answer during our time in Peru was whether I was "spiritual enough." God had helped me grow in a much-needed sense of balance—and not just for riding flimsy boats on the Amazon. I learned about balancing kindness with firmness, spontaneity with schedule, and a sense of purpose with a sense of humor. I learned to not sweat the small stuff as I swatted mosquitoes out of the kitchen while I cooked and chased rats the size of cats out of the bedroom. And I fell in love with the freedom of jumping into the back of a pick-up truck to go to church, running to the market on a moto taxi, and taking siestas with Lydia in our bunk bed of one hammock suspended over another.

"Before I come home, I need to paint a clear picture of myself," I wrote in my last prayer letter to friends and family in the United States. "Put two inches of mud on my shoes. Rub a little dirt into my shirt. Have sweat trickle down my cheek. Put a confused look on my face—I'm trying to understand Spanish. And knock off any halo you may have pictured over my head. I am no more perfect than I was the day I left. One truth about missionaries is that they are not glorious, super-spiritual, super-human people. They laugh, they cry. They misunderstand. They understand. They work. They sweat. "

In my quest to find God's place for me, I realized that missions work is not for perfect people in impeccable situations. It's for those who offer their hands to be used, as Lynn Porter did by signing for the deaf despite the physical limitation with which she was born. And it's asking God to let sinners like me learn from beautiful examples of humble service what it means to be clay in the potter's hand.

And the amazing truth is that He does.

The Nadine Hennesey Story

Ed Hennesey and Nadine Terrill on their wedding day, July 1, 1989, in Xenia, Ohio.

Nadine and Ed by the shore of Lake Huron during a youth group bike trip shortly after they were married.

The House of Laughter in Mitrovica, Kosovo.

A Hennesey family outing in Ontario, Canada, when Lydia was nine months old.

July 1992, Lydia and Nadine enjoying a Terrill family picnic at Highland Park, New York.

Nadine and Lydia at a small village on the Amazon River in Peru.

adine and Lydia aboard a boat with
eir good friend Julie for an excursion
own the Amazon to teach vacation Bible
hool in a river village.

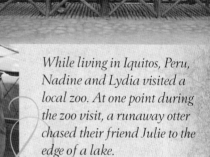

While living in Iquitos, Peru,
Nadine and Lydia visited a
local zoo. At one point during
the zoo visit, a runaway otter
chased their friend Julie to the
edge of a lake.

Nadine
and
Lydia
pause for a
picture while
enjoying a pic-
nic with a visiting
team from the US at
the House of Laughter.

Natasha Donaldson and Lydia, Nadine's two remarkable students, perform a Christmas program in Peru.

Lydia helps Armando put together a model car at the House of Babies in Albania as Nadine observes.

Irida working on a craft shortly before she was adopted by an American couple.

In February 2001,
Nadine and Lydia visit the spot where the House
of Laughter would be built in Mitrovica.

Nadine teaches an English class at the
House of Laughter.

Reading books in English helped the children pick up the language.

Three House of Laughter graduate Fidaim, Fisnik, and Nehat take in the circi with Nadine. It was an appropriate outin because "Teacher" claims that all thre could at times be "class clowns

Summer camping in the Rugov Mountains meant student-prepare meals cooked over a campfire. Burr or not, it always tasted grea

Lots of basketball was played at the House of Laughter. Controlling emotions and including others were two key life skills taught on the HOL court.

Students and teachers enjoyed hiking the mountains in the mornings, playing volley-ball in the afternoons, and singing around a campfire in the evenings.

Lydia competing in a puzzle competition with her HOL friends during a birthday celebration.

Nadine may have been "Teacher," but she couldn't let the young people have all the fun, so she did some repelling and rock climbing too.

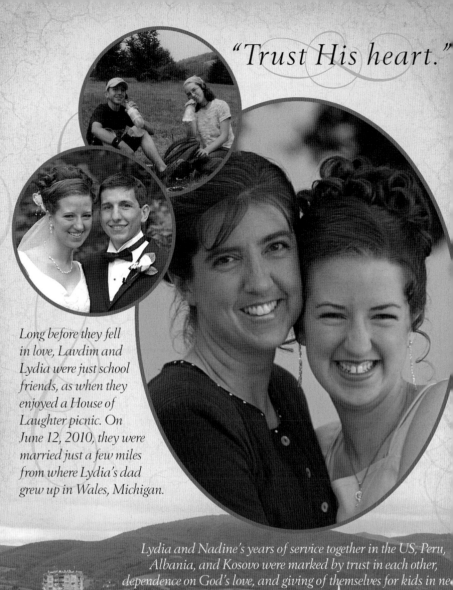

"*Trust His heart.*"

Long before they fell in love, Lavdim and Lydia were just school friends, as when they enjoyed a House of Laughter picnic. On June 12, 2010, they were married just a few miles from where Lydia's dad grew up in Wales, Michigan.

Lydia and Nadine's years of service together in the US, Peru, Albania, and Kosovo were marked by trust in each other, dependence on God's love, and giving of themselves for kids in ne

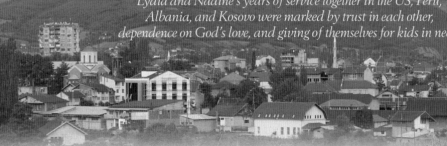

In Mitrovica, Kosovo, a city divided by sectarian and religious animosity, the House of Laughter and the Kosovo Leadership Academy were designed to help young people grow academically, socially, and spiritually.

8

The Argument

"I shall be telling this with a sigh
Somewhere ages and ages hence:
Two roads diverged in a wood, and I—
I took the road less traveled by,
And that has made all the difference."
—Robert Frost

The test was over, and it seemed that everyone involved had passed.

Lydia's happiness and safety had been my first concern in going to Peru. If at any time she had seemed overwhelmed or unhappy, we would have returned early. Although the test wasn't really for Lydia after all, she had aced it and come back to the States taller and stronger, tan and athletic. All those hikes up and down the mountains had to count for *something*. She was happy and confident, learning she could jump into situations that looked "iffy" and land on both feet. Her mind had been opened to other cultures and her heart to people in need. Besides that, her Spanish was great. When Lydia talked about her adventures in Peru, her friends back home asked their parents if they could go too.

I treasured my Iquitos family in Christ, and I could easily go back and live among them. My love for the Peruvian people, especially the children, had not diminished. There was no problem with where we had gone or what we had done. It had been challenging, for sure, but energizing. In the genuine enthusiasm I had expressed over our experience in Peru, I realized that I had given my family and friends every reason to assume we would be going back.

The next logical step in our future was for me to attend candidate school. The ABWE staff had reserved my place at the annual training sessions at its headquarters in Harrisburg, Pennsylvania, so I could pursue that possibility. Everyone was happy for me—and I think relieved—because my life finally seemed to have some direction. I didn't want to tell them that at a much deeper level I didn't have it all together.

I couldn't tell anyone else—not even my family—that there was something I wasn't sure about in all this. I was still taking baby steps in learning to trust God in *everything*.

"I know there's a purpose in life," I had written after returning from Peru. "I was taught that you follow God wholeheartedly, and He will give you the desires of your heart. And the greatest desire of my heart was to be Ed's wife and serve with him. But now that's impossible. I'm having a tough time trusting. I always thought that giving God my life meant 'I'll go anywhere . . . do anything You want me to do.' I didn't think it meant doing all that but with a big empty place in my heart. I'm afraid to give it all."

The week before the conference in Pennsylvania, I drove to my parents' home, where Lydia would stay while I was gone. Still struggling inside, I prayed for God's direction. There was a big difference between honoring my husband's faith with a year's experiment and trusting God with my entire life. I knew from experience that I could easily fall into a pattern of going through the motions by staying busy for God while holding my heart at a safe distance. But I needed more in life than that.

The night before I was to leave for Pennsylvania, my car stopped working. My lack of mechanical knowledge hinders an accurate description, but here was my problem: My car wouldn't go anywhere. *Maybe this is a sign,* I thought.

That night I pulled a Gideon kind of request. "Lord, if You do not want me to go tomorrow, then leave the car as it is. If You want me to go tomorrow, You'll have to fix the car tonight." This was a pretty big fleece—I knew that. The next morning I packed the car, turned the key, and listened as the engine roared to life. I had no option now but to leave for the nine-hour trip to Pennsylvania. God had fixed my car. It ran smoothly the entire way.

The first person to greet me in Harrisburg was my friend, Barb, the woman who had answered the phone a year earlier when I made the call about short-term teachers. She gave me a hug and explained the training schedule for candidates who already knew where they hoped to work, but then she added that on the third day of the conference we would hear representatives sharing details of new areas of service that had been approved in the previous eighteen months.

When we got to the last presentation of that session, I listened as missions leader Phil McDonald said, "We work closely in the communities where specific people groups are jeopardized by current political or social issues." He then began listing professional workers for which the organization had immediate need. "Engineers, architects, lawyers, doctors . . . ." Just at the point where I felt I had no qualifying skills for these positions, the last role came up on his PowerPoint slide. "Orphanage directors."

I leaned forward, my mind already seeing pieces of the puzzle line up. Since coming home from Peru, I had checked into the possibility of applying for a leadership role at the orphanage introduced to me by my friend Julie—the place we had gone to on Saturdays when I was in Peru. That position had been filled.

Phil's wife, Becky, finished the presentation.

"The need is great," she said. "Children have been abandoned in the streets. Many have been abused, and all are left either to starve or find ways to survive—ways like becoming thieves and prostitutes. And those born with physical or mental handicaps are especially vulnerable," she added.

"But I need to be honest," Becky cautioned. "Anyone who considers orphanage work in these areas should have both eyes open to the risks involved. Some of these countries are at war or suffer ramifications from recent wars."

The moment the session ended, I hurried out of the room, battling the racing of my heart against unsettled issues.

I started walking. When I got past the parking lot, I kept going, walking up and down the tree-lined hill at the edge of the conference grounds, arguing with myself. Half of my brain urged me to admit how passionately I wanted to be a part of life-changing social and spiritual intervention with needy children. The other half slammed to a stop and asked me if I could really believe that anything—*anything*—God asked me to do could truly satisfy at this point in my life.

"Can it really be true," this part of me challenged, "that you can walk through the loss of someone you love so dearly, and have so much grief, and yet God could still give you the desires of your heart?"

"Yes," a voice from somewhere responded.

"All my life I wanted to do something that would make a difference," I reminded myself. "Like George Mueller and Amy Carmichael did. All those times growing up, when I read about them and their work with orphans, I wanted to have an impact like that.

And then there's Elisabeth Elliot, I thought, remembering the letter she had written to me. *She was a widow too . . .*

"So do you still want to be like them?" the other voice pressed. "Or are you just going to sit around feeling sorry for yourself?"

"But I'm not a great hero of the faith," I countered, remembering how I had struggled to sleep after Ed's funeral. I recalled that when I did sleep I had a nightmare in which I had seen myself slapping Christ across the face.

For months I had been so hurt I couldn't open my Bible or even pray except by writing my words, as if they were someone else's. During those dark days and bleak nights I had envisioned the people whose cruelty had put Christ on the cross, and at one miserable moment of recognition, I had, for the first time, seen myself in the picture.

How could a sinner like me deserve to be used by God—and why should He give me the desires of my heart?

Broken by my own unworthiness, I had asked God to show me the work He had for me, one that matched the circumstances of my life. Going to Peru had been a test—a way of sticking out my finger to touch the dream my husband and I had shared. The appeal to which I had responded had been for a teacher, and that's what I was—a single mother with a passion for education.

Today, for the first time since Ed's death, I felt that I could see dangling in front of me what I was meant to do with my life. Working with orphans had been a desire of my heart since I had been a young girl. Suddenly verses I had memorized as a child came into sharp focus. "Trust in the Lord with all your heart and lean not on your own understanding; in all your ways acknowledge him, and he will make your paths straight." This passage was more than a great motto for a wall plaque. It was the crisis moment I was in. And I sensed that, in a Robert Frost sort of way, I had the opportunity to take "the road less traveled by" that would mark the rest of my days.

God had given me a heart's desire once—my husband—and had taken him away. I wasn't angry anymore. Even though what God had done was impossible to understand and hard to accept, I had experienced His faithfulness. But if I said yes again, would He snatch this away from me too?

Either God was worth trusting totally in a way veiled to me, I saw as one clear alternative, or . . . .

"Or You're a liar," I said out loud.

Suddenly weary, I sat down on a bench under some trees. And in that moment, I sensed that God, with His still, small voice, slipped into my argument. "So the question's not really about you, is it Nadine? Do *I* pass *your* test? Do I?"

Only God heard my answer. Even if there had been anything left to say, it's hard to talk when you're crying. For a long time, I sat there, weighing human experience against grace. One you can accomplish on your own. The other you simply accept, unconditionally, with no checklist. Could I trust God with the journey even if I couldn't see the map?

That night I called home and asked to talk to Lydia. "There are some children who need someone to love them," I began. "We could do that, couldn't we?"

Lydia agreed, as if that was a silly question, and then asked how soon I'd be home. "I miss you, Mommy."

"I miss you too. Just a couple more days," I promised.

I missed Ed too. That would never go away, but for the first time since he died, I knew that I could let go of his dream, pick up the little girl he had given me, and start on the journey God had planned for us.

In my mind I saw a young mother rocking a baby in the dark, desperately asking God to hold them both. "Sleep sound in Jesus," I had sung to my newborn. "Sweetheart of my heart . . . the dark of night will not keep us apart. When I lay you down in your bed for the night, He holds you gently 'til morning is light."

"Thank You," I whispered. For the first time in my life I understood the value of losing an argument. And hearing God win.

9

PUSHING OPEN THE DOORS

"You can give without loving,
but you cannot love without giving."
—Amy Carmichael

"To ward off the spirits of those who have died," our Albanian driver, Miguel, said matter-of-factly, speaking through the translator sitting next to him.

I had asked him about the scarecrows, some with skulls attached, hanging from the rafters of house after house we passed as we drove from the airport to Vlore, Albania. To me, scarecrows were for the garden, but to the Albanians, I began to understand, they were part of a protective superstition. Although Miguel seemed to accept these specters of death as an inevitable part of the landscape, they struck me as a sad symbol for life in a country often caught as the turf between warring factions.

"A factory once," was Miguel's answer to my next question as we passed one of many large crumbled brick buildings with every window blown out. "But not today," he continued, explaining that farming was now Albania's main source of income. And yet, during our three-and-a-half hour drive through the countryside, it seemed odd to see only one tractor—though our van was passed by one Mercedes-Benz after another. When my mental tally hit 100, I asked Miguel how there could seem to be so much wealth for some and so little for others. "It's crazy over here now," he said, shrugging his shoulders. "The thing is with those cars—probably only one was paid for. The others were stolen."

Hearing Miguel's slant on things fleshed out the history I read before leaving the US but had not really understood. While under communism, the European nation of Albania had been called the world's "first officially atheistic country." Religion was superfluous, the Communist dictator had told his people while assuring them that Albania was the richest country in the world. With the fall of state communism in 1991, both lies were exposed—resulting in the frantic jockeying for power between social, economic, and political powers that made life feel, as Miguel put it, "crazy over here."

Embarking on a working tour to observe orphanage administration in different cultures, seven-year-old Lydia and I were scheduled to spend June and July 1998 in the southern coastal city of Vlore, Albania. My sister, Sheri, had joined us for the first month. To finish off the trip, in August Lydia and I would visit a faith-based humanitarian program to aid children in India.

Primed by the memory of needy children in the orphanage in Peru, I had checked to see if it would be appropriate to bring a gift of supplies. With the contribution of friends, we loaded four extra suitcases that had, amazingly, arrived with us at the airport. I thought we might lose them yet, though, during the five police checkpoints we passed at which vehicles were searched for various reasons—to verify documents, assure no weapons were being carried, and so on.

But we were stopped only at one. And when the officer asked what was in all of our extra bags, I gave him the simple truth, hoping he would believe me.

"Diapers . . . and toothpaste and soap. And crayons. "

The policeman slammed the door and motioned us on.

When we pulled up in front of The House of Babies, a three-story building in Vlore, Miguel helped us out of the van. A young Italian woman with dark hair that was pulled back under a bright blue scarf hurried out the door and extended her hand to us. "I'm Beta," she said motioning to herself. "Welcome."

She glanced at her apron, sprinkled with flour, and smiled. "I have been working in the kitchen." Sheri, Lydia, and I followed Beta past the guard in the doorway and into a dark, cool hallway. The directors had gone home for the evening, Beta explained, but would be back tomorrow. She had volunteered to wait for us and show us to our room when we arrived. As we stood outside the kitchen while Beta hung up her apron, suddenly a young girl bolted down the hall and clasped my hand.

"Friendly, aren't they?" I started to say to Sheri, when my attention was jerked back to the girl grabbing my shoulders, then my hair, and climbing over me like a ladder to reach for the electrical fuse box on the wall behind me. Beta stepped out of the kitchen, calmly pulled the child down, turned her around, and motioned her to go upstairs. "That is Irida," she said. "Now, let's take care of your suitcases and get you settled."

The House of Babies, she explained, served children from infancy to age seven as a recent partnership between the government and a ministry called Advancing the Ministries of the Gospel (AMG), in which minimum expenses were funded by the state. Its doors were open to little ones whose parents had been killed or had died from illness. But Albanian law also allowed parents who could not care for their children to leave them at an orphanage, though some of these were claimed later, Beta explained, "when they are old enough to work in the streets." Many of the children cared for had physical and mental disabilities, and because the directors knew what the children would face if sent to another facility as exceptional cases, they were kept here as long as possible.

"Sometimes children are left at our gate," she concluded. "This morning the bell rang, and we found a baby wrapped in a blanket with a paper pinned to it. 'Christopher,' is all it said."

The next morning Beta took us for a quick tour of the facility. A warehouse in the basement stored clothing and other donations. On the first floor we were welcomed by Amalia, the Albanian director, and Peter, who was filling in while the American director was in the States. Albanian workers and volunteers stopped what they were doing to greet us as we walked past the kitchen and dining room on the way to the stairwell.

The second floor was where the children four and older lived. As Beta opened the door of the room where they all played, I saw a few children watching the television against the wall. Others ran all around them while some sat alone on the floor, passing time in their own little world, it seemed. On the third floor we saw one room for the babies, with row after row of cribs, and another two rooms were full of toddlers.

We spent the rest of the day coming alongside the other workers, trying to learn the daily schedule. We started by holding and playing with the babies. Then we walked to the beach on the beautiful Bay of Vlore with a group of the older kids. After we came back, we helped with the babies again and then had lunch. That afternoon we mixed up sugar dough and brought in two children at a time to help us cut out the cookies. At snack time we served the cookies, and then we took the kids outside again in small groups. At eight o'clock dinner was served, the older children went to bed, and we took one more round with the babies, meeting the workers who would stay all night.

As we settled into the routine, I began to sort the kids out by name—and by the way they acted. Irida (the little girl who used me as a ladder the day we met) was in my group to walk to the beach one day. At one point she saw a little boy with an ice cream cone. Irida jerked away from me and headed toward him. As I ran after her, I watched her use different "persuasive" tactics—first she pushed him, and then she knocked him down. By the time I caught up, she had grabbed the cone, opened her mouth, and crammed the whole thing in. At least she's determined, I thought, pulling her from the boy. But I was determined that she wouldn't keep acting this way.

"Survival of the fittest" was the accepted mode, we were beginning to see, as the children, who ranged in age and mental ability, all jostled for attention. Some days we were able to channel their energy better than others; what really concerned me, though, was the way they pushed and hit one another—and us—to get their way.

One day, as we were serving lunch, a six-year-old named Eni threw her bowl of soup on the floor. Lydia walked in at about the same time with a tray of Jell-O for the kids. Eni grabbed the tray and started to reach for Lydia. I quickly slipped between them, blocking her. With Lydia squarely behind me, I knelt down and looked Eni directly in the eye. She stared back blankly, without saying a word. Then she yanked on my hair—pulling out a handful.

The next morning a worker brought Lydia a newborn kitten as a way, it seemed, of apologizing for what had happened. That night I watched my daughter feed her pet with an eyedropper and hoped it would live. She needed something to love that wouldn't hit back. After Lydia and the kitten went to sleep, I wrote in my journal.

"The kids were brutal to each other today. They would come up and smack you as hard as they could and beat on anybody, no matter how big or small. Jumping on the trampoline, a little boy who was obviously mentally disturbed, pulled down his pants, urinated on the other children, and then ran around, laughing and screaming as he tried to pull down the other kids' pants. I realize now I have an unrealistic view of orphans. I thought they would all be sweet little children with big, sad eyes."

My sister Sheri's optimism helped my perspective as we washed our clothes one morning. It was five o'clock—a good time, we discovered, to get a load in because, even when the building had electricity, the wash cycle took two hours. Besides that, I needed to feed the kitten. "At least we have washing machines," Sheri said.

"That's where they used to wash diapers," she continued, pointing to a filthy, broken-down claw-foot bathtub against the wall. "Beta said that when she came five years ago, the workers would throw the diapers in there and stir them with a stick to wash them."

We knew the task facing the staff was huge, even though working conditions had improved under the new leadership of AMG. No children were currently in the process of being adopted, and later that day we heard that three more had been dropped off from another orphanage. One was an infant who had been found in a plastic bag in the trash. Another baby had been given up by her fifteen-year-old mother. And the third baby was skin and bones, with a huge hump on the back of his head.

That night we volunteered for an extra two-hour shift, giving the third-floor night worker a break. We helped settle the new arrivals, and then we walked through the quiet rooms checking each crib. "Hello, Sarah," I said as I picked up a six-week-old who was lying in a puddle of milk that had dripped from the bottle propped next to her on a towel. I fed Sarah the rest of her bottle, and then Lydia rocked her to sleep.

We began making progress logs with goals for each child. It might be a note about muscular development—something as simple as suggesting a target date for when a baby who had previously been tied in a bed might be able to sit up. Rudina was a seven-month-old with Down syndrome, but even though I had only seen her lying in her crib with her arms and legs sprawled out, I sensed she was more alert than she seemed. I started exercising her legs, and when I turned her on her tummy she raised her head and reached for a toy.

For most of the older children, there were complicating emotional issues. The boy we had seen jumping on the trampoline, wetting on the other children, was nine, but he had only been heard to speak once. "He seems to be caught in a shell," I wrote, "and when I take him outside to play ball, he only wants to throw the bat over the wall and then escape himself." One day he did run away, and Sheri found him running down the road outside.

And then there was Irida. I wanted to help her but was confused about how to start. The director had hired a special needs teacher, Mira, who told me details that completely changed my perspective. Irida, who was now eight, had lived in the orphanage all her life. As a baby she was diagnosed by a government doctor as having "very little brain activity," and so she had been treated as stupid, Mira said. For her first three years of life, Irida was strapped into a big wooden crib, day and night, with four other babies who slept tangled all over each other.

"Things are much better now with the new director and his wife," Mira added. "They put the children in their own beds. That's when I knew Irida was smart. She took her blanket and tied each end to the sides of her bed to make a swing!"

In the playroom, the children began to show hints of trust—fragile little Mercida, who was eight but looked like a tiny doll, smiled and started singing every time we saw her. Others would reach out their arms for a hug or help going down the stairs. Sheri and I alternated between working in small groups and one-on-one interaction. While one of us played a simple math game with a few children, the other would help a child draw a picture or put a puzzle together. Before long the children began to take pride in their work. They loved to find their pictures hanging on the wall among the fast growing art collection. The milestone was when Eni—who had pulled out a hunk of my hair shortly after we came—came over to me, took my hand, and led me to a place to sit down. Eventually she walked away, but I knew we had made a start.

Meanwhile, Lydia developed her own approach. She wanted the children to have fun, so she got permission to take the younger ones, who had never been anywhere but on the third floor, on short trips outside every morning. Two at a time, she took them to play on the swing set inside the enclosure, and every half hour she would come back to get the next pair. The older kids began to hang out in the big classroom in the afternoons, waiting for Lydia to come back so they could play dodgeball and other games. It was their favorite part of the day.

One issue I had faced back in the States while in the process of raising funds for the trip to Albania was whether there would be "sufficient opportunity to share my faith," since I would be working for a humanitarian facility run by the government. As the days in the orphanage passed, the answer became increasingly clear.

Shortly after we arrived, as we were struggling to read an Albanian Bible I had found, two housekeepers came along and gave us a language lesson. For the next hour they pronounced the Albanian words, and we did our best to come up with the equivalent in English. One verse we covered was John 3:16. The Bible is considered "beautiful literature" by the Albanians and encouraged as a valuable addition to the language lessons. The children wrote Proverbs in glitter glue and proudly hung them on the wall with their pictures.

We received invitations to visit our co-workers in their homes, and conversations opened on a more personal level. From the start we had been told that we were free to share our faith as people asked questions. And they were asking! "Albania has very few Christians," I wrote in a letter home. "Out of the fifty-two Albanian workers, eight are young believers. What an opportunity to rub shoulders with forty-four families who are not familiar with the gospel of Jesus Christ. Now, that is a good-sized church!"

The most pressing confirmations, though, were the children themselves. As our two-month Albanian tour came to an end, I tried to capture my observations. "I looked at pictures of the orphanage before help came along five years ago. One picture stood out more than the others. It was a picture of Mercida. She was three years old and weighed four kilograms. It was terrible! God cries for children like her. Should I have to defend my legitimacy as a missionary while children like Mercida die every day? What does Jesus want me to do? He wants me to be His arms and to hug them for Him. Jesus wants me to love them the way He loves them."

"Dr. John," the beautiful dark-haired children of India called the humble man as they crowded around him. He was the man described in the literature I had read as "the founder of India International." With a personal welcome to India, Dr. John David began our tour of the orphanages and schools by telling us his own story, revealing the roots of his passionate connection with the children around us.

A native of India, Dr. John was eleven months old when his father died. There weren't good medical facilities in their village, he explained. Desperately poor, his mother struggled to find work, taking any jobs she could find. But as a widow, she faced many obstacles. She heard about a mission school for girls, applied, and was hired as a school teacher. While he was a young boy, John lived with his uncle.

While serving in the army, John was on his way to deliver a message when the fuel in his bike ran out. He stopped at a village meeting place to use the phone, and he overheard the pastor inside ask a question, "What does it profit a man if he gains the whole world but loses his own soul?"

The question haunted him until he accepted the Lord as his personal Savior. He became an evangelist, traveling from place to place with only the clothes on his back.

Through his ministry, Dr. John met a young medical practitioner, Dr. Satyavedam, who was also dedicated to serving the needy. The unlikely marriage of a highly educated young doctor to a poor evangelist in 1955 led to a life together of shared compassion. The couple dedicated their lives to a holistic ministry to help meet their country's social, emotional, and spiritual needs.

For the next three weeks Lydia and I had the opportunity to see some of the dimensions of this outreach. We opened our eyes to take in every possible detail of a wide and varied landscape of care. The orphanages, all staffed by nationals, focused on specialized needs—coordinating schools, living compounds, and medical facilities into what looked like small villages. From a large central facility, a cooking staff prepared meals that were collected and delivered to the surrounding schools where they were served, still hot, to over four thousand children every day!

Because the national workers invited us to join them, we had the chance to see their ministry close up. The first day after we arrived, we visited a hospital specializing in eye care. I was allowed to don surgical scrubs and watch the physician skillfully remove a cataract from his patient's eye. When he was done, he turned to me and put the brown cataract in my hand. His hand was steady; mine was shaking.

We put on aprons and delivered steaming hot lunches in some of the schools, ranging from elementary to college. One school had so many children that some had to sit outside. At a high school, we were invited to watch a special program in the gym, and we were blown away by the talent of the students! Some performed singing and dance numbers in beautiful costumes, and others did karate and gymnastics routines. Academics got the spotlight then, with a demonstration of science fair projects. Afterwards, we were invited into the classrooms, and at break time, went outside to ride a camel, adorned with its own costume. I've ridden a lot of horses, but that was the only time I've been on a camel. All I could think of was a roller coaster in slow motion.

Wearing lovely saris and head coverings that Dr. John gave us, we were invited to several special gatherings related to the community health and education programs. At a conference held in the meeting space at the back of Dr. John's house, I met and shared my testimony with more than 200 national pastors and teachers. At another service Lydia and I sat cross-legged on the floor with the women and listened as they sang with drum and tambourine accompaniment. At our going-away dinner I spoke as an "American representative." It occurred to me that since such meetings typically featured speakers reporting on foreign investments, Lydia and I were undoubtedly the poorest guests they'd ever had!

The orphanages under Dr. John's management offered practical hope for desperate situations. Some young people had been rescued from sex trafficking. "Survival" for many of them, prior to intervention, had been offered only by serving as temple prostitutes.

One of the site visits that touched us personally was also a day of unexpected celebration. On August 17 we had devotions with some of the India International staff, and we then walked over to a special school, called Ebenezer. Lydia and I joined the others in helping to serve steaming hot lunches to the children, and then someone announced that we had a special dessert. They had made a huge birthday cake because Dr. John, having misunderstood me the day before when I said it was my brother's birthday, thought it was my birthday. "Oh, that's all right," he laughed when I told him. "We will celebrate your brother's birthday today!"

Lydia and I sat down and were immediately surrounded by a circle of children. It was a hot day, and some of them fanned us with pieces of cardboard while another little one kept blowing in my face to help me cool off. We played a game, and then they tried to teach us some words in their language. Their consideration touched our hearts as being more than polite—the boys and girls expressing concern for our welfare all had polio.

Afterwards we visited and gave treats to the elderly ladies who lived on the campus because they could no longer stay with their families. And then we took a treat to the housemothers as a way of thanking them for caring for the children 24 hours a day. Before each gathering, Dr. John prayed for the people present and for my brother, David, celebrating his birthday. I silently thanked God for all of my family, who played such an important role in why I was here today, with my daughter, listening to the head of India International pray for my brother.

The visit that affected me most profoundly was to a leprosy camp. I have to admit that what we saw there was nothing like my pre-conceived expectation of sad-eyed people holding out their hands for a bit of rice. Instead, we entered a joyful gathering of hundreds of lepers seated under a large tent, women to the left and men to the right. A program was already underway as we walked down the center aisle. Girls danced and sang, and afterwards a gospel message was given. It was a privilege to be asked to share a word of encouragement with them, but their encouragement to us was profound. Their faith was vibrant. They had been excommunicated from families as the "untouchable caste." They had body parts missing from the effect of the disease. They had no earthly possessions. Yet they were joyful. John David said that those who were believers had told him they were glad they had leprosy because that is how they came to know Jesus. "And what is my excuse for unfaithfulness?" I wrote in my journal that night.

The opportunity to visit India opened my eyes to a revolutionary perspective on leadership within its cultural setting. Hundreds of workers were mobilized into teams that achieved dynamic results. I had seen people trust God for vision and strength—and then these same people went to work as His hands and feet by feeding thousands of children. These little ones are not a social burden to Dr. John David and his staff. They are individuals with bodies, minds, and souls. And they are the future of India.

"John David has become a new hero for me," I wrote as our tour ended. "One I've had the privilege of meeting personally. He is India's George Mueller."

Just as a coach pulls the team into the locker room to replay key moments of the game, I came home at the end of our summer ministry tour and tried to sort through our experiences. In India I had seen how God had provided work for a bereaved mother and her son, John, and had then led that young man and his bride to love children of their country as Jesus would. In Albania, God had used our positions as a widow and fatherless child to tell others about Him. "How can you have so much joy?" one of the Albanian orphanage workers asked one day, stopping me in the hall to talk. "And how is Lydia so happy?" What could possibly soften the hearts of women like this, I thought—women who had toughened themselves against the reality of pulling deserted babies out of trash bags? It wasn't my "educational objectives" or anything I could give on my own. God's care for widows and orphans was more than a promise; it was the unexpected nudge that opened hurt-encrusted doors of the heart, from the inside.

Behind each of these doors was a real life painting of beautiful children, some with dark skin and hair, and some, like my daughter, with light features . . . all with need and every one of inestimable value.

Life is short, and I longed to become part of the picture of hope I had seen—and as soon as possible. With the fast-changing political climate of our world, I knew that some doors of opportunity that were open might close soon. It was time to run. As hard as it is it is for me to ask others for financial support, I knew by then that God was in charge of details such as money. My commitment could no longer be "short-term, part-time, maybe, maybe not."

I couldn't wait to get back.

10

ONE CHILD AT A TIME

*"You never really know a man until you
stand in his shoes and walk around in them."*
—Harper Lee, *To Kill a Mockingbird*

Our flight back to Albania in 1999 progressed with what seemed like one miracle after another.

When we left the United States, the airline agent informed us that only half our luggage, crammed with supplies, would arrive in Greece. However, when we stepped off the plane every piece was there.

Before we began our journey from Greece to Albania, we were told that the border between the two countries had been closed because someone had hijacked a bus and killed some passengers. We had no problem leaving Greece, but we encountered a problem upon trying to enter Albania. The border police refused to stamp our passports unless, he said with no explanation, we gave him forty-five dollars each.

I turned to look at the team of eight college students who had come with me—concerned about what this unexpected charge would mean to them.

Thankfully, the American director of the House of Babies orphanage, Mark, was there too, and he was well versed in the negotiation process with border police. In a quiet, non-threatening way, he communicated that we were in no hurry. After a moment, the officer stamped our passports and waved us through.

With that, we were on our way to what would become home for Lydia and me.

It's one thing to travel around the world for a short mission or survey trip and then to head back home, but it's quite a different story to travel around the world knowing that where you land will become your home. This time Lydia and I approached the House of Babies orphanage, where I would be teaching, without return airline tickets in our suitcases. As we arrived, my pulse rate increased, and the doubt began to creep in, "Is this really what I want to do the rest of my life? Is this best for Lydia? Should I have brought this team of college students with me when I still have to figure out what I will be doing?"

As I walked down the hall of the orphanage, weary from airplanes, crowded vans, and dirty, bumpy roads, I heard someone call my name. "Nadine, Nadine!" squealed nine-year-old Mercida, sticking her head out the door of the cafeteria where she had been eating lunch. I threw down my bag and knelt on the floor as the little girl who still looked far too small for her age ran into my arms. "Listen," she said eagerly, and she began singing something we had taught her the year before. "God is so good . . . ." I hugged Mercida back as she sang, my doubts gone. A year ago we had come to "the orphanage." Today I was back with children whose names and lives were already woven into my heart.

The team jumped into twelve-hour work days in shifts of caring for the babies, playing with the older children, organizing clothing donations, and doing some light repair projects. Every night after supper we all met on the flat roof of the orphanage. Under a canopy of stars we talked through the next day, sang, and prayed. Then we had a quick game together before turning in.

One night shortly before the team was to leave, the students expressed their desire to thank the orphanage staff. Along with the directors, we hosted an appreciation dinner for the Albanian workers. I don't think anything like that had been done for them before. Saying goodbye to the Cedarville missions team gave me a vision for how energy, love, and productivity are multiplied by a group like that, and I prayed that others would come in the future.

Lydia and I set up our home in a little apartment next to the orphanage. I rented the room next door to use as a classroom, where I started teaching school for the older children from the orphanage. I also used it to teach English classes for kids from the neighborhood. A woman who lived in a nearby apartment stopped me in the street one day, complaining because so many children came to my class—she said they waited outside and caused "problems." The next day, ten minutes before class was to begin, I heard yelling on the street and stepped outside to see what kids were causing the problems. The students were standing there, waiting, while five women in a circle next to them yelled at each other. When one of the women saw me, she walked over, still yelling. I couldn't help smiling because she was talking so fast I couldn't make out a word she said. Before long she started laughing, and the women all walked away. But ten minutes later they were back, standing at the door with their own kids. I smiled again and welcomed my new students.

In the early afternoons, Lydia and I worked on her lessons, and in the late afternoon we went back to the orphanage to help with dinner, play with the kids, and love the babies.

"I'm writing this by hand," I began a letter to my supporters after returning to our apartment one night. "We have no electricity at the time, so I'm using a gas lantern. Sometimes I get a little too intent on what I'm doing. I lean forward until I hear—or smell—my hair start to sizzle, and then I sit up straight again. I want you to come with me to visit the children on the third floor. This is the best place to relax after a day of teaching. Little three-month-old Viola and Flavio, her twin brother, lay waiting, wrapped up in their beds. They look a little bigger than when we first came, but that's because they're wearing four outfits to stay warm. I wish you could hold them, snuggle them, and kiss them. Moving on, you would see Anri still lying on his back, as always. His muscles are drawn so tight he can't straighten his arms or fingers. Although he is two and a half years old, he cannot sit up or walk. I know you would smile at his laugh as I hold him and skip and sing up and down the hall. In the next room, the two-year-olds toddle around. If you start to sing, they would surround you and as many as possible would climb into your lap. The toughest part of the day is leaving.

"I have fun listening to the older children at night when they're supposed to be sleeping. The boys are on the right side of the hall and the girls are on the left. Last night I heard one of the girls, Pavlina, call across the hall to her brother, Armando. 'We will now sing,' she announced. 'Jesus loves the little children of the world.' Then, up and down the hall, as if in music class, a choir of children joined in. These moments make teaching worth it all."

When the time came for a visit from my field advisors, Phil and Becky McDonald, I made plans for a run to the airport. Nani, the orphanage driver, asked if he could combine the trip with some other errands, so our route took a few extra twists and turns. Nani's final errand was to deliver a letter to an office in Tirana, but he didn't know where it was. He parked the eighteen-passenger Mercedes van, gave us instructions to wait there, and disappeared down the street. Lydia and I waited—and waited—entertaining ourselves with songs and guessing games. It was now twenty minutes before we were to pick up Phil and Becky. Suddenly three police cars and two motorcycles surrounded our van. "Maybe we're illegally parked," flashed through my mind.

"Where is your driver?" an officer asked me in halting English.

"He left awhile ago," I began. "Can you explain what is going on?"

"What's going on?" the officer repeated as he slipped into the driver's seat. "Your driver is—." He searched for the word, gave up, and started again. As he talked—partly in English, partly in Albanian, and all very quickly—I got bits and pieces of the story. Meanwhile, we received a full police escort to the station. I felt like we should make the most of this little parade and wave at all the people staring at us as we sped by.

At the police station the van was inspected, and we took off once again, with Nani back at the wheel. I couldn't help but laugh about the whole thing as we drove to the airport, but if I had known the whole story, I would have kept my laughter to myself, at least in front of Nani.

It wasn't until a few days later that I learned—through an English translation of our adventure—what actually happened. After delivering his letter, Nani had gone back to where he thought he parked the van, but it wasn't there. He panicked, thinking it had been stolen. He hurried to the police station and reported the van as stolen and, with it, two missing Americans. That's the word the police received over the radio, and interpreting that to mean we had been *kidnapped*, launched a rescue operation and searched until they found us—right where Nani had parked the van.

One of my compelling desires from the year before was to help Irida, the child who had climbed all over me the first day we walked into the orphanage. Because she was deaf, Irida had spent her early years being treated as if she could not think for herself. But Mira, the special needs teacher, took a special interest in Irida and began providing the attention this child desperately needed. Irida was ten now, already past the age to stay at the orphanage. "If Irida is not adopted soon," I wrote back to my supporting churches, "she will go to an institution where she will be physically, mentally, and sexually abused.

"She is not a 'project' however," I added. "She is a little girl with a sharp mind, understanding, and love."

I knew Irida was frustrated by being locked up inside, unable to communicate with others. If she wanted something, she grabbed it. If she did not like what was going on, she threw herself backward to the ground. To let you know she wanted to play ball she would bang her head on the bat. The only sign language experience I had was a class I had taken at church back home, but with several books I brought with me, I decided to try. Irida and I could learn together. Two of Irida's first signs were "please" and "thank you." Once she mastered these, she became Miss Manners of the orphanage—even if she had to smack you on the arm to get your attention so she could gesture, "please." Eating was Irida's favorite activity (though you would never know that by looking at her), and once she learned to thank God before starting her meal, she became the fastest signer I had ever seen!

Irida's quickness with learning sign language opened her world. She learned signs for thirty-six animals. The other students thought it was fun communicating with her in this new way, so for the first time in Irida's life, she began "talking" with people instead of just hitting them. She quickly improved in her school subjects and went from scribbling to drawing people and houses. In math, she advanced from adding single digit numbers to adding three and four digit numbers. Her progress in the classroom and her growing joy in life caused staff members to stop, smile, and hug her. The beautiful part was, Irida started to hug back.

In April, I asked for permission to let Irida live with me in the apartment five days a week for one month while Lydia was in the States visiting family. I wanted to see how she would function in a real home.

The first week was a struggle because Irida didn't know what to do in a house. She stayed so close to me I called her "my shadow." The bathroom was my only place of solitude. "She watches my every move," I wrote in my letter about her. "She sees an activity once and knows how to do it." One day I carefully ironed a craft project, then unplugged the iron and put it away. When I walked back into the room a few moments later, there was Irida, ironing *her* project—along with the plastic tablecloth.

Inside the apartment, Irida became fascinated with mechanical things. She would sit mesmerized, watching the front loader washing machine. One day she picked up a screwdriver and motioned, "How?" I showed her how the tool fit in the slit of a screw and gave her a piece of wood and three screws for practice.

The next day she watched as I struggled to open the top drawer of my nightstand. "Forget it," I said to myself and walked out frustrated. A few moments later Irida ran after me, grinning and waving the screwdriver. She grabbed my hand and pulled me back to my room. What was left of the nightstand lay in pieces by the bed. She had pried the entire top and side off. However, the drawer was now opened and I could get what I needed. "Good?" Irida signed, looking at me expectantly.

"Good," I signed back. "Very good."

"Shadow" progressed to finding projects on her own. A new thing she enjoyed was taking showers. She had never been required to wash herself until she lived with me. One day, as I was in the kitchen preparing a cake, she went around the corner to the bathroom. When she hadn't come back by the time I put the cake in the oven, I went to check on her. Opening the bathroom door was like stepping into a cartoon! Bubbles were everywhere—all over the walls, the floor, the ceiling! And by the tub stood a little human statue made out of bubbles, holding out an empty shampoo bottle. "Clean?" she signed, smiling as she blew bubbles off her lips.

I wanted to increase Irida's opportunity for social interaction beyond the home environment, so every day we walked into town and took the bus home. In the beginning, Irida had very little confidence. She shuffled her feet, hung her head, and made a lot of noise. But frustration released her stubborn streak. If she got mad, or didn't want to walk any more, she would sit down in the street or wherever she was and refuse to move. Once a man stepped onto the bus and sat across from us. His elbow was bandaged and the rest of his arm was missing. Irida pointed and laughed at him, and though I stopped her immediately and shook my head at the man apologetically, I understood. *Isn't that what she's learned?* I thought. *Isn't that how she's been treated her entire life?*

The toughest part of having Irida come stay was taking her back to the orphanage. The first time we returned to the orphanage, she threw herself on her bed and began to rock violently back and forth. Another time she ran away, and I discovered her sitting on my doorstep. *She needs a family*, I thought as we walked back again.

A few weeks later a letter came from a family in Ohio. They had followed Irida's progress in my letters and wanted to adopt her. Along with the official application, they sent a photo album of their family. How do you explain what "family" means to a child who has never had one, I wondered as I tried to prepare Irida for her new role. Every day we looked at the photo album, signed each person and thing, and attempted to define each one. I pointed to the woman in the photo, writing out the word "mom" and stroking the side of my face.

Irida patted my shoulder and signed back, using the same gesture.

"No," I signed and pointed to myself. "*Lydia's* mom, your teacher."

"Brother" and "sister" were easier, but explaining "dad" was hardest of all. I wrote out the word, signed, and pointed to the man in the picture. A dad protects you, I tried to explain, holding a doll close and gently covering it with my hand. Irida looked from the word to me and then to the photo, and then shook her head.

The day Irida's new parents were to arrive, I had trouble concentrating on my morning classes. At lunchtime, Irida and I walked together to the office. She was ready—I hoped. She wore a new dress from the donations stored in the basement, and her hair was washed and pulled back in a ribbon. She sensed the excitement around her. When I saw the couple down the hall with the director, I knelt in front of Irida and opened the photo album. "This is your mom and your dad," I signed. She turned and her eyes widened as she saw the people in the picture walking down the hall toward her. Soon we were face to face. I signed again, "This is your mom. This is your dad." Irida squealed with delight and threw her arms around both of them.

I thought back to the day I first met this girl, with her hair flying in all directions and unwilling to let herself be touched. I looked at her now, as she stood between her new mom and dad, a different child. She's beautiful, I thought, and not just because she's clean and has a new dress. She was happy. God sent Irida a family to love her the way He loved her. I think she understood.

Seeing the hope in Irida's eyes as I said goodbye made it even harder to look into the eyes of two of our other children. Six-year-old Armando and his four-year-old sister, Pavlina, had been born into a clan of gypsies, or "Roma," which I had learned to be the more respectful descriptor than "gypsy." They had been dropped off at the orphanage by their mother several years before, with the legal provision that she could reclaim them at any time. In such cases, as long as children are visited by a family member—even for a few minutes once a year—they are not eligible for adoption.

It had been over a year since anyone had visited Armando and Pavlina, which meant that legally they had been abandoned, and the staff was eager to place their names on the adoption list. Lydia and I talked it over, and I inquired about adopting them myself. Time was running out in another way, because when the brother turned seven he would be reassigned to another orphanage, and his sister would go with him. Although the deadline for their mother to claim them had passed, our Albanian director, Amalia, told us that the family had to be informed and given a certain amount of grace time.

So Amalia, Lydia, and I set out for the Roma camp. On a desolate stretch of land strewn with trash, the people lived as outcasts, clustered in clans. We found Armando and Pavlina's family clan, huddled together under a shelter—none of us could call it a house—a ragged structure of material stretched and held together with metal strips. All the relatives came out when we arrived. They were thin, dressed in several layers of clothing, had teeth missing, and even the youngest were bent over from the grind of life as they knew it. The children's mother was in town trying to collect money, they told us, and maybe we could find her there. We started off the way they pointed, and after another half-hour's search a woman with a toddler perched on one hip sauntered over to us. She was holding another child by the hand, was pregnant, and yes, she said, she was the mother of the children in the picture we held out. Cigarette dangling from her lips, she told us she would come for them, then turned and walked away.

Without speaking, I listened, and left praying she would back down. But on the last possible day, she showed up to claim her possessions. Armando sat in my lap whispering, "I don't want to go," and Pavlina clung to Lydia's arm, crying. As we sat there together, the woman began to talk quickly. Pointing toward me she told the orphanage director that if I wanted to help her children I could. If I gave her enough money to build a house, she said without a trace of emotion, I could keep them. In this Albanian's mind, every American is rich. I sat there, waiting for the right words to come to me.

"We don't buy children," Amalia said, speaking for me. The woman reached for her son and daughter and dragged them out of the orphanage.

"Now Armando and Pavlina beg in the streets," I wrote in my journal that night, with a battle raging in my heart. "Why is it children are always the ones who suffer?" I was angry at the system and sad for little ones who had heard their mother barter for them, as if haggling for meat in the market.

Filled with what I felt sure was righteous indignation, I fumed for days. Why would God allow this woman to have such wonderful children when she didn't even care about them? But God began prodding my heart, exposing my selfishness. As hard as I tried, I couldn't escape the mental image of the first time I saw her . . . standing there, kicking the trash aside, holding two little ones and another on the way, with no husband to support her. Outside their own camp the gypsies were targets of verbal and physical abuse. She probably wasn't treated better than the trash at her feet.

"I began to think about how Jesus dealt with people," I wrote another night as my own child slept. "He talked to the woman by the well in Samaria—a woman who had five husbands and probably a few 'Armandos and Pavlinas.' He talked to her because he loved her. She didn't know what love was until she met Jesus. This gypsy woman is like that—how can she love her children when she doesn't know what love is?"

I was drawn to go back to the Roma camp to visit the children I had hoped to adopt—and their mother. Not as an orphanage worker planning to negotiate, but simply as a friend. Being there didn't change my indignation at a social system that valued its children primarily for what they could steal or sell, including their own bodies. What had changed for me was God's nudge to love unconditionally, knowing I would receive nothing in return. I wanted to be kind to this woman, marginalized by an oppressive system, because that's what Jesus would do.

She was a human being who understood what it meant to feel hopeless. I had felt hopeless too, in a completely different way. For the first time since the day I had walked into her world, I began to feel what it might be like to slip into her shoes.

"Sometimes I wish I had 100 lives to live," I wrote after one of these visits, "in order to meet the cries for help I hear every day."

11

LAUGHTER IN THE HOUSE

"The deepest joy in life comes from giving to the neediest people."
—Wendell Kempton

"Could you come help us?"

Even if he hadn't said his name, I would have recognized the voice over the phone, for it brought back memories of my first visit to the Albanian orphanage more than two years earlier. Peter Hoffman had temporarily filled in as administrator then, relocating later to Mitrovica, Kosovo, to begin a relief ministry for families left devastated from the recent civil war—providing food, clothing, and shelter. Women whose husbands had been dragged away or killed were now struggling to raise children alone.

"And the children—" Peter said quickly, describing the plight of kids who wandered the streets. The proposal date for starting a project to help the kids was the following January. "Could you come and help us?" he asked again. I appreciated his ministry, I told him, and wanted to stay in touch about it, but I was already committed to a school-year program in the Albanian orphanage that ran through June.

When Peter called again later with the possibility of a slightly delayed start, I again declined. Besides teaching in the special needs classroom, I was still working through details of the adoption of a little boy who had heart problems and needed additional care. It wasn't a good time to move, I explained.

After Christmas, Peter came to visit in person. As we sat together, this man of short stature and huge passion looked at me and spoke directly. The Albanian-Serbian pattern of reprisal and revenge had escalated into violence that had shattered families and had damaged or destroyed several schools. Now that the violence had subsided, survivors were struggling to rebuild their lives. In Mitrovica, Peter told me, he and his wife currently delivered food and clothing boxes to 487 widows and 1,162 children under the age of eighteen who had lost one or both parents. His vision was to build a learning center in Mitrovica, designed to offer a nurturing environment in which to offer classes and help children gain direction for life. Most significantly, Peter said, the date for finishing the building had now been delayed until August. The first possible date to open the learning center was September 2001. When he prayed about the director for the center, Peter said, God had brought me to mind, and nothing had changed that. Would I consider coming across the border to help?

I'm not sure I heard everything accurately after he mentioned the change in starting date, because my mind was racing. All of a sudden the inner struggle I had felt since our first conversation had somewhere to go. Although Lydia and I had grown very close to the children and staff at the orphanage, the dynamics there were changing rapidly. God had graciously blessed us with a dramatic increase in adoptions. In the next month alone, six of our children would leave to join new families! On a sad note, we were also saying goodbye to several other children who would be forced to move to a state orphanage within the month. Only three of the 38 children I had been working with might still be in the facility the next year. The average age of our children had dropped from between four and five to two. The role for which I had come, as a teacher, was changing. The position in Kosovo, it seemed, was all about education. And now, with the new start time, I could honor my current commitment and still be involved in the new project. The only nagging doubt in my mind now was how Lydia would feel about leaving.

"We'll come to visit," I told Peter. "And we'll pray about this. That's all I can promise."

A soft mist hovered in the air on the morning in February 2001, as Lydia and I jumped into the old red VW van outside the orphanage. As the mist turned to a cold rain, Lydia snuggled next to me.

"Just a quick trip—right?" she had asked as we packed our suitcase. Although I sensed that we were taking the first step in a new direction, Lydia was reluctant at best. Month after month, she had been next to me at the orphanage, holding, feeding, changing, and loving babies. She had taught toddlers to walk and had played with the older kids. They were the only brothers and sisters she had, and she wasn't about to pack up and leave them. We were both quiet as Miguel began our three-hour drive from Vlore, Albania, to the airport in Tirana—passing over roads that looked like a NATO bomb had strayed off course and hit the highway. As we rode I prayed that by the time we came back after the weekend, we would know what to do. Both of us.

When we arrived, Miguel dropped us off with our single suitcase and waited while we ran inside to confirm the flight. "Everything is set to go," I said when we came back, relaying what I had been told. Miguel took off to return to Vlore. By airport regulation, we had to stay outside the terminal until closer to boarding time, so Lydia and I found chairs under the canopy of a coffee shop and settled in for what should have been a short wait. Lydia entertained herself by designing dresses on her sketchpad, stopping every now and then to ask which design I liked best. After several rounds of judging, I went to check on the flight and saw "Delayed" posted next to our flight number. After checking again several times, with no change, I asked the attendant at the counter what was happening. "The flight is delayed," was all he said. Finally, two hours after we should have taken off, I received a different answer. "The flight has been cancelled. Come back tomorrow."

Now what? We couldn't stay at the airport, so I looked down the long row of eager taxi drivers, picked one, and asked him to take us to the only place I knew in Tirana, the Stephens Center. It had a nice restaurant, I remembered, and a few rooms to rent—so perhaps this would work out as a fun break before trying again at the airport the next day.

After lunch, Lydia and I went to the front desk to check on room availability.

"I am sorry," the lady at the desk answered. "All the rooms have been booked. Is it just the two of you?"

"Yes. Could you recommend a hotel?" I asked.

"The two of you can't stay alone in a hotel," she said, shaking her head. "That's too dangerous. You can stay with my parents."

"No, thank you," I answered. "That is very generous, but we will be fine in a hotel room."

"No," she insisted, "you will stay with my parents. Give me five minutes, and I can have everything wrapped up. I'll take you to my parents' house. You will be safe there."

I never did find out if there was something happening that I had missed or if she really was just concerned about us as a single woman and little girl, but I decided that she knew more about being alone in the city than I did. That night Lydia and I found ourselves sleeping on the floor in a home of complete strangers, a couple in their eighties who treated us like family. They fed us, made sure we were warm, and arranged for their son to drive us to the airport the next morning. "Guardian angels?" I wondered as we thanked them for their hospitality.

Relieved to see that our flight was on schedule, we boarded a little twin-engine plane and took off for a thirty-minute trip to Prishtina, the capital of Kosovo. Forty-five minutes later—a third of which we spent flying in circles—the passengers around me began to get edgy. One of their frustrations was that although this was a foreign airline, filled with Albanians, the flight attendant and pilot spoke English. Lydia and I could understand, though, what the other passengers discovered only when someone began shouting out a translation. The Prishtina airport was closed due to ice. The people flying the plane knew that when we took off, but they hoped it would change. It didn't.

"Maybe we weren't supposed to go on this trip, after all," I said to Lydia, as we headed back to Tirana.

"But Mom," she said, drawing it out as she always did when something was really important to her, "I want to go to Kosovo."

"You said you didn't want to go."

"I changed my mind."

Back in Tirana, we sat with the other passengers in the airport for two hours, took off again, and this time landed in Prishtina, where the ice had been cleared from the landing strip. I was sure that with the delays no one would still be there to meet us, but as we stepped out of the airport, there was Peter, standing in front of the crowd. He grabbed our suitcase and drove us to his home in nearby Mitrovica where his wife, Maria, had a warm meal waiting.

Next, we went across the street to the house where we would be staying for the weekend. It wasn't used much, Peter explained, which was why it was almost as cold inside as it was outside. But he had already started the coal-burning stove, he assured me, so it would thaw out soon. Some neighborhood children knocked at the door and asked if Lydia could go sledding with them, which was something she couldn't do in Albania. She stood still just long enough for me to bundle my coat over the one she was already wearing, and then she ran outside to play with her new friends. Meanwhile, I chipped away at the ice that had formed inside the window.

The next day we visited the site of the new project. At the moment it was a concrete slab surrounded by two big bombed-out buildings and another one that had been salvaged and was full of refugees. People who had lived in the north side of the city but could not return to their homes because of ethnic hostilities had taken up residence there.

As the construction chief described the plan for the learning center, I could see it too. The rubble surrounding us only heightened the need for a clean, attractive symbol of hope. Later that day we toured the south side of Mitrovica, a city separated into ethnic groups. Walking on the main streets and sidewalks, we saw soldiers with their AK47s. Their armored tanks stood nearby. Trash and barbed wire were everywhere. The city, in its damaged condition, was not attractive, but the people walking its streets were. They greeted us warmly and offered to share the little they had. Yet behind their generosity of spirit, the struggle for survival was etched on every forehead.

The morning we were to fly back to Tirana, Lydia woke up at five o'clock with food poisoning. Thankfully, the airplane trip took only 30 minutes this time. We grabbed a taxi and headed back home—stopping along the side of the road several times so Lydia could throw up. Flight delays, freezing weather, and food poisoning, I thought, reflecting on our "quick trip." It certainly wasn't anything like the February ski trips our family used to take—complete with a cozy cottage fireplace, beautiful scenery, and mugs of hot chocolate. To be honest, the trip Lydia and I had just finished had been terrible in those terms. But as glad as we were to pull up in front of the orphanage in Vlore, we were also just as sure that it would not be our home much longer.

I hate goodbyes.

It helped that we weren't moving until summer. We filled our days with special times with the children at the orphanage, and we went twice to visit our students who had been moved to a different location. In June two energetic mission groups came to the orphanage. A five-member ABWE Impact team came early in the month, joined by nine Cedarville University students including my brother David. The group was led by my other brother, Troy, and my sister, Cindy. It was a blast having them with us. They packed the month with extra classes, activities, and special attention—all adding up to happy memories for the children and a smoother transition than we had anticipated. We waved goodbye to the Cedarville team (except Cindy, who stayed to help us move) on the last day of June.

On July 4, 2001, Lydia and I made a cake, decorated the playroom with balloons, and celebrated my birthday by having a party for the kids, just as we had the year before. Before tucking the children into bed for the last time that night, we gave each of them a picture Bible, told them how much we loved them, kissed them, and said goodbye.

Lydia and I struggled as we looked into the eyes of these little ones we had come to love. No more rocking them to sleep. No more jumping on the trampoline with them or walking them to the beach. No more school lessons and taking a break by sitting under the fig tree, talking and eating figs until we were sticky with juice. Looking over the past two years, the joys far outweighed the struggles. We had walked many miles together and learned to love each other in special ways. Although we had explained our new assignment to the children, we knew that some did not understand that when they woke up in the morning we would be gone. Lydia and I understood, and our hearts ached as we hurried home to cry.

At five o'clock the next morning, we climbed into an old, green German army bus that was already packed with our belongings. The good roads from Albania to Kosovo go through Macedonia. However, because of warnings we received and some recent problems along that route, we decided to take the dirt road over the mountains directly into Kosovo—an interesting 14-hour drive.

As the bus raced around the first couple of treacherous curves in the road through the mountains, all of our boxes of supplies, which were piled in the back of the bus, began to topple down on us. I spent hours with my back braced against the seat in front of me and my feet against the boxes. My only hope was that we would get to Kosovo alive. We did!

God kept us safe and even paved the way through customs. From what I knew about the charges to bring donations for the orphanage across the border, I expected to pay up to $200. But when all was said and done, I paid just $7.50 with no hassles from the customs officers.

When we arrived at our new home—an apartment on the grounds of the learning center still under construction—we opened the door and saw nothing but walls and a floor. There was no kitchen, but thankfully, there *was* a bathroom. Cindy made bookshelves and a shoe rack from doorframes left in the warehouse. Friends who had just arrived to work at the technical school, which would adjoin the learning center, installed our kitchen from bits and pieces we found. Another Cedarville team, led by Scott Huck, came in late summer and helped with final construction for the center, putting in floors and window frames. We wouldn't have made it without them.

Anticipating our September opening of the House of Laughter, my to-do list was huge: visit homes, design the program, write the curriculum, find and train a staff, and invite the children. Starting with a twenty-page list of widows and widowers, I began searching for students by knocking on doors. The first woman I met apologized as she opened the door, inviting me inside the broken-down hotel that was her home at the moment. Apologizing again she explained the smell—sewage filled the basement. As she served tea, I began asking the questions on the brief survey I had prepared. She answered politely, and then interjected her own question—"Why did you come to Kosovo?" When I shared that I was a widow with a fatherless child, and that we had come to help, her story tumbled out.

As I listened to her, taking notes for our records—"six children . . . husband beaten in front of their house . . . watched him die . . . no hope of change," I began to sense a message meant for me. "Give me a ministry that matches my circumstances, even those I didn't choose," I had prayed after Ed died. Perhaps my connection with a relief organization had encouraged her to open the door to me, a complete stranger. But the key that opened her heart had nothing to do with what I could offer—it was the common bond we had as widows, as single mothers. From that place of mutual understanding I asked the question, "What is it you hope for most for your children?" Her answer came freely. "Education. A good education to help them start again."

A journey of grace had brought me here. I loved to teach, and I couldn't wait until the learning center was finished and ready to open. But I also longed to support the broken families struggling at home by bringing light to the despair that shaped their world. I wanted them to find a purpose for surviving the heartaches they faced.

By the end of the summer I had hired a staff of Kosovar teachers, cooks, guards, and other workers. The curriculum was ready for classes in English, literature, life skills, math, drama, art, and character training, along with an hour in the gym each day for sports. Students were registered for half-day shifts, as a supplement to the condensed times they could attend their regular schools because of the shortage of buildings and teachers. Depending on whether they came in the morning or afternoon, a hot lunch would be provided daily to end or start their time with us. On selected Saturday mornings we would open for games and service projects.

On September 15 the mayor of Mitrovica cut the ribbon, and we celebrated the official opening of our learning center, the House of Laughter. Lydia and her American teacher, Stacey, dressed as clowns and passed out balloons to our guests, including international soldiers. Our original goal had been to begin with 100 students in first through eighth grades, but when we started classes on September 17, 180 kids walked through the doors and sat in desks delivered three days before. The kitchen and gymnasium weren't finished yet, but by then we knew that flexibility was the word of the day, so we happily served lunch in the library and played soccer in the front lot.

"When the door opened, we entered this building," one of our first students, a sixth grader named Merita, wrote later in a creative writing assignment. "It was a new beginning. And today I am still learning new things and having fun with my old friends. I will never forget the first day at the House of Laughter."

The facilities God provided—four classrooms, a library, an office, and a gym and kitchen/dining area in the works—were a great blessing, it's true. But what was happening inside is what made the House of Laughter special. From the moment kids burst through the front gate, we wanted them to feel God's love in action. They were accepted as they were, free to share their ideas and dreams, and encouraged to move beyond grief and anger to hope.

As with any new venture, there were kinks in the system to work through. In the beginning, we had to cope with the noise of helicopters hovering over the school, an inconsistent electricity schedule, and an undependable water availability. Our first winter, we had no central heat; the few wood-burning stoves helped some, but most students sat through classes with their coats permanently attached.

We were watched constantly by soldiers on the hill above the property. I knew they were there to guard us, but we didn't find out until later that we became a great source of entertainment for them. There was a close call one day, though, when we scattered the kids about on the lot for an obstacle course—complete with clues about how to run the course. We cheered as they pushed each other in wheelbarrows, climbed through ladders, and ran furtively from one place to another looking for hidden clues. While we were having fun, the soldiers watching with binoculars from the hill above were trying to figure out what was happening. They thought we were beginning special training drills, and they were about to come check things out—we later heard second-hand—when the game ended and everyone lined up to go inside.

Being in charge as a director was a new experience, and it stretched me—especially as I tried to understand a different culture and fine-tune my growing Albanian language skills. It kept me on my knees, always thankful for what had happened that day. And sometimes very thankful for what had *not* happened.

Our staff of four local teachers played an incredible part in creating the learning center's creative atmosphere and feeling of family. Our art teacher, Arben, who also managed the library and helped coach sports, was in charge of painting and decorating the library and foyer. As the kids came in, they saw enormous pencils hanging from the ceiling, Mickey Mouse pictures on the walls, and splashes of bright color everywhere. Iset taught journalism and literature. He also spent hours playing soccer and basketball with the kids and becoming a mentor to the young men without fathers. Remzije, our math teacher, worked patiently through her lessons and then tutored the children in small groups until they could move to the next level. She made them feel valuable by offering time outside of class to sit and listen to their stories. The geography and life-skills programs were taught by Flurije, who was raising her own nine-year-old son after her husband died and her father was killed during the war. Flurije had carried her son on her back across the river when they fled to a refugee camp.

Our non-teaching staff were family too. From bean soup to chicken and rice, Zylfije and Sadete made lunch delicious. They cooked, cleaned, and served as though they were doing it for their own families. The guards greeted the students as they arrived and said goodbye as they left. After school, they occasionally joined us at one of the picnic tables near the gate for tea and informal language classes.

The children were easy to love yet challenging at the same time. There were some power struggles (what did I expect, I asked myself, considering the fights they had gone through to hang onto basic things like a piece of bread) and impulsive responses. There were times during those first few pace-setting, laying-down-the-rules, and "don't-think-I'm-kidding" days that I collapsed in my office and asked what I'd gotten myself into. But for the most part I could hardly contain my excitement. As my mind raced to keep up with the lessons, songs, and games planned for each day, I watched the children. Most seemed so eager to be here that they could hardly stay in their seats. I kept thinking back to their home history interviews.

One thirteen-year-old and his younger brother and sister had hidden in the mountains with their mother during the war and then fled to a refugee camp. When they returned, they lived in a tent for two years.

Another little boy and his sister began living with their 82-year-old grandmother after their mother (who was now in a mental hospital) killed their abusive father.

A young teen whose father was declared missing during the war lived with his mother and brother in a one-room house behind the garbage company.

A twelve-year-old girl whose mother died a year earlier was responsible for caring for her five younger siblings.

These and other stories we had recorded on the students' registration forms supported the cry for help that had drawn me to Kosovo. But as I listened to the kids talking and playing together,

I heard something else I wasn't expecting so soon. It was something I had longed for as I sat in the sun on a hot day two months before, watching construction on our building, wondering if we could make a difference in the grief around us. "We were like those who dream," I had read as I opened my Bible to Psalm 126 that day. "Then our mouth was filled with laughter."

It was already starting. The most beautiful sound I heard when we started classes at the learning center was the kids' laughter.

12

They Call Me Teacher

"The teacher is the one who gets the most out of the lessons,
and the true teacher is the learner."
—Elbert Hubbard

My students often teach me more about life than I teach them.

Irida, my deaf student from the Albanian orphanage, still comes to mind when I find myself banging my head against the wall (and not always figuratively) over the inevitable frustrations that come with a new job in a new place. It's almost funny how my mental image of Irida begins to take on features that look and sound a lot like me. "I can't do this. I won't. You can't make me."

When Irida was learning sign language, we had progressed to the point where I would give her give her something only if she signed for it. This reinforced the sign and rewarded her at the same time, and for the most part it seemed, she liked the plan. It worked, and it actually took a lot less energy than her former tactic, which was to throw herself on the floor and have a fit until someone gave her what she wanted.

One afternoon we were sitting in the kitchen working on adding three digit numbers with the concept of carrying. Irida was hungry and she kept looking at the snack I had placed on the counter. I knew exactly what she wanted, but she wouldn't ask for it. So I wouldn't give it to her. She howled, scribbled on her math paper, and threw her pencil. I held out my hand for the sign. She threw herself on the floor. She knew I was waiting for her to ask properly, but she refused to do it. I wanted her to understand she could not control me with her misbehavior, but I was getting frustrated. After nearly an hour of this battle of wills, I got up and walked out of the room. But I left the door open. Keeping her in my line of vision, I saw that she was watching too—looking from me to the snack and back again. *How stubborn can she be?* I thought. *She knows I want to give it to her, but she won't ask!*

At that moment it was as though God said, "I know exactly how you feel. You are the same way. You want something from Me, but you do everything you can to get it on your own. I want to give it to you, but in your stubbornness you miss out because you do not ask."

Humbled, I walked back in, sat down on the floor next to Irida, and waited again. But not long. When she signed for the food, I reached up to the counter, grabbed the plate, and set it in front of her. "It's all yours, girl—enjoy."

It's not easy to put into practice what Irida taught me. It feels that there's a lot more up to me as I struggle with people over cultural misunderstandings, deadlines, lost documents, or "how can I possibly raise enough money for this project?"

But sometimes, just before I throw myself on the floor, I remember. *If you want something, don't waste your time doing all sorts of things trying to get it. Start by asking for it.*

Before we opened the House of Laughter, I started asking for help. I asked God to give the kids who came to us not only an education but also joy, and He did, but not without some "sowing with tears" along the way. The political climate in Kosovo shifted randomly, like the occasional hand grenades tossed just close enough to remind us that dissension was still alive. "Now nothing is normal," one of our seventh-grade girls wrote. "There is no work. It is very hard to graduate from school. Life is difficult without happiness, but I think one day it will be better."

Most of our young students were polite and seemed eager for life to get back to normal. Just as you would see flowers springing up around piles of bricks left from a recent bombing, they *wanted* to move on. But for others, trauma was so close to the surface that a hint of tension triggered bursts of aggressiveness. I remember watching them suddenly start to push each other during games, and then become defensive and pull back from being touched. Some of the boys were often disrespectful to girls. And when the train transporting Serbian workers went by, a few automatically ran to the fence and screamed out their hatred.

How does this work? I asked myself. *How do you take these individuals with their own broken hearts and struggles, most looking inward, and help them look outward to see each other?*

As a teacher, I was eager to come alongside these children and teens who had lived through crisis and longed for hope. My daughter enthusiastically jumped in among the students as a friend who became a sister. Our creative staff exercised diverse gifts, and a steady flow of mission teams multiplied our energy. And underlining everything we did was the love of God that permeates shattered lives. Day after non-stop day we opened our doors and students hurried in. And somehow, in ways that still amaze me, the House of Laughter became a place that felt like home. We became a family.

The first students who came to us have graduated now, but we often meet for a bite to eat or just to talk. "Teacher," they still call me.

"Teacher, do you remember the day I threw a rock and hit my friend on the head?" Fejzullah's random question popped up one evening as we talked.

"Oh, yes," I said. I remembered the urgent run to the doctor's office, the stitches, and the home visit explaining to the injured boy's father what happened. "I remember."

"I was so afraid you would kick me out," Fejzullah—or Fez, as we called him—continued. "If you had, I don't know what I would have done. The House of Laughter is where I could go and just relax and think and eat and read and play without any pressure."

Fez had a rough start in life. By the time he came to the learning center as a second-grader, his father had been married several times. Taken from his birthmother, the boy had been shifted from one stepmother to another. When he was four, he suffered a sudden case of appendicitis. His father's wife at the time—who resented caring for the child—threw him to the floor and kicked him. Emergency surgery saved his life, but the long scars on both sides of his ribcage are a reminder of that terrible day and his long stay in the hospital.

Fejzullah's life became unexpectedly hopeful when his father married again, this time to a woman who took Fez in and cared for him as part of a growing family. But when the war escalated and his father was killed, Fejzullah's newest stepmother, who felt she couldn't care for the boy and her own young daughters, sent him back to his birthmother. She, in turn, signed off—saying she wanted nothing to do with him. That's when he was referred to us.

As Fez made friends at the center, his confidence and energy grew. But if conflict started, even during a game, he retaliated. The day after the rock-throwing incident, Fez came to my office. He knew he had messed up, and he said he was sorry. I accepted his apology, and then we talked about the beautiful gift of God's forgiveness. The story was completed though, in an unexpected way three days later when the father of the injured boy showed up at my office. The other teachers and I didn't know if he had come to complain or even demand money. But surprisingly, he had come to thank us, he said, for what we were doing. He knew from experience how hard it was for the kids. He wanted Fejzullah to know that.

Fez is a young man now, still trying to figure out life. "I learned to respect others at the House of Laughter," he told me as we walked down the streets of Mitrovica, "and got directed on the right road." I hope he knows that he'll never outgrow the love and friendships that started there. I think that's why he still shows up often at my door. I think he still needs a little touch of the House of Laughter. He needs his family.

One of the best things I learned from my college education professors was that learning isn't limited to the classroom. In our mission statement for the House of Laughter—hammered out before there *were* classrooms in the learning center—I included service projects designed to promote personal and public responsibility. Opportunities for "trust, flexibility, patience, and stamina" became reality through sports and group activities. A big part of the security the center offered came from working as a team. I was firm, it's true, and it didn't take long for the kids to memorize my policy: "If you break the rules, you have to live with the consequences." They needed to learn how to live within boundaries, and by boundaries I didn't mean barbed wire fences. They knew all about that. I meant honoring authority, respecting one another, and taking care of things even if they didn't belong to you. I meant, "No, you can't smack somebody in the head just because you're mad."

The learning center weekly schedule was filled with classes, and we worked hard. But every month we looked forward to at least one special activity—from talent shows to treasure hunts, Olympics to obstacle courses, basketball tournaments to birthday parties, and singing contests to skiing. That's where the real bonding happened. That's where I would notice things as a mom would—such as the amount of time a kid could go during a ballgame without losing his temper. Also, I had observed that most kids kept their personal stories to themselves when we interacted in the classroom. But now and then, as we sat around the campfire or hiked together or crashed after a crazy game night, something would come up in conversation.

It didn't take long for our weeklong camping trip to the mountains of Rugova (what I call Kosovo's Swiss Alps) to become the summer highlight for our junior and senior high students. The first item of business after jumping off the bus was to pass out garbage bags and clean the campsite. Then we split into groups to put up tents, set up the kitchen, and mark off the field into sports areas. When the work was done, it was time for fun. Afternoons were for games, sometimes organized and some just as free time. The kids threw Frisbees, played football and volleyball, and had golf competitions. Every morning after breakfast we spread out across the field for a few minutes of quiet time before coming back together to reflect on God's creation and talk about where we were going in life. Then it was time to pack up and take off for the day's morning hike. Sometimes it was a casual walk with lots of talk along the way and stopping to wade or swim. But the favorite and most challenging hike was up the mountain by the lake. We used a buddy system, and we told the kids that the important thing was to take one step at a time, without rushing.

"Whew! Maybe this wasn't such a good idea," I thought to myself one year as we headed up the steepest part of the mountain climb. "Everyone take a five-minute break," I called to the front of the line as I tried to catch my breath. Merita, one of our graduates who had come on this trip as a leader, was with me at the back of the group.

"This reminds me of the war," she said, making herself comfortable on a nearby rock. For seven years Merita had been my student and Lydia's close friend. But this was the first time she shared her personal story with me.

She explained how her family had walked at night through the mountains, trying to reach safety after leaving their home. Merita was seven years old then and had two older sisters, two younger brothers, and a younger sister. "Suddenly my father would motion to us to sit quietly," she said. "Then we would hear the voices of soldiers in the nearby trees. When all was quiet again, we would start walking slowly up the mountain, not speaking a word. We hid during the day." I looked up the steep path we were struggling to climb now and thought about what it must have been like for a child to climb in the dark, knowing that unfriendly soldiers were nearby.

Shortly after their escape through the mountains, Merita's mother died because of a combination of physical complications and a lack of medical care. Merita loved her mother very much and had a difficult time after her death. She knew her mother had already made several sacrifices so her children could have a good education, and she was determined to continue that dream. When the doors of the House of Laughter opened, Merita was there to register as a sixth-grader.

After her junior year in high school, she was one of six who qualified for Leadership Educational Development, an intensive training program and outdoor adventure. Her greatest challenge was rock repelling, she told me, but once she took that first step off the side of the mountain, she loved it.

Merita has taken a lot of challenging steps since then. She attended the University of Prishtina, where she majored in English. During that time, she and I sat across from each other in a coffeehouse, and I listened as she caught me up on details about her classes. Suddenly she stopped mid-sentence. "Thank you, Teacher," she said. "I would not be where I am today if it were not for the lessons I learned at the House of Laughter."

What lessons had she learned? I asked myself. *Keep your eye on the goal and take the first step. It might be dark and steep—maybe a step of faith. Take the next step, and the next.*

We began the learning center with the goal of reaching and supporting the widows who sent us their children. During home visits the first summer, I kept thinking that the widows needed a chance to get out and have fun together, just as their children did. In the second year we were in Kosovo, I invited the women to form a weekly group. About twenty-five of us began meeting in the House of Laughter kitchen on Sunday mornings. We drank tea, talked, and read a psalm from the Bible. And knowing how they loved to knit and crochet, I encouraged them to bring their needlework with them. I was amazed at their ability to work with four needles at the same time and never drop a stitch no matter how fast they were talking! It took all my concentration to work with one needle, trying to manage the one stitch my grandmother had taught me—the single stitch I had used to make a scarf for Ed (which he never wore in public).

The ladies watched me laboring to hook the needle through and around the yarn. "You are so quiet and slow. Are you sick?" they asked. Out of my comfort zone (I kept hoping that just once they would ask to meet in the gym to play basketball) I smiled and listened as the ladies talked. Over time, their conversation began to turn from war stories to what their children were doing and what was happening now. Our kitchen became a very noisy place—which I liked—and not just from twenty-five women talking at the same time. The best part was that they were laughing too.

Some of the women hadn't learned to read, they told me. A friend of mine with literacy training visited, wrote two workbooks for the women, and then trained my staff on how to assist them. Another need all the women talked about was financial. Most of them were supporting their families on the equivalent of approximately $60 per month. We talked about the idea of a small business, but with classes and activities for the students filling my days, I didn't have time to start this venture. That's when Carol Prime stepped in.

God brought Bill and Carol Prime into our team as part of a related ministry in Mitrovica, and they quickly became part of the House of Laughter family. Bill came over to the center and repaired bikes that had been donated for the kids. Carol and I began talking about the widows' program as we walked in the morning for exercise. She was fun to be with and had great ideas for things the women could do. So I asked her if she would take over as leader of the support group. Along with spiritual support and friendship, Carol encouraged the widows to market their incredible needlework. By selling their homemade lace tablecloths, doilies, purses, and other items, the widows made a modest increase to their meager incomes, enhanced their sense of dignity, and contributed to other ministries for orphans.

God kept sending special people, and our staff grew. We hired a young man named Sefidin to help with technological support. The widows found another great friend when Beth Cooley joined our staff as young teacher. I first met Beth when she came on a student team to Albania; she joined us in Kosovo later and then came full-time. She had a heart for our students and the single mothers. My sister, Sheri, came back to teach as well, after coming on a short-term basis, and she strengthened the English program. An ever-welcome flow of mission teams from the US and other countries invested time and energy that helped us keep going. They taught, coached, organized day camps, helped with construction, directed plays, and took part in our worship. One team set up a dental clinic in the Primes' living room. As varied as the groups were, their common bond was that even if they came in feeling like tourists ("What water is safe to drink?"), by the time they left, they were family.

"Teacher," another one of my graduates still calls me. Blonde, blue-eyed, and *always* laughing, Fisnik leans over and lightly pushes my shoulder. Invariably he will tease me—reminding me of times he and I have made fools of ourselves trying to take on a challenge like skiing down an ice-covered mountain. His tone is almost never serious, yet he is unexpectedly tenderhearted.

I remember the night of his graduation from the House of Laughter. Everyone else was ready to walk in, but Fisnik wasn't there. Impatiently, I looked at my watch. "Five more minutes," I said out loud. Suddenly I heard laughter in the hallway and in walked Fisnik, surrounded by three bodyguards and a cameraman, obviously bribed for the occasion. He might be late, the look on his face clearly said, but he was going to have fun.

In his early days at the learning center, Fisnik involuntarily visited my office often because of his language choices. Half the time I didn't even catch the actual words (my Albanian wasn't that subtle yet), but I could tell by the other kids' expressions what was going on, so I would send him to the office. One question I learned to ask in those cases was "Would you use that language if your mother were standing here?" And Fisnik, who loved and respected his mom, would shake his head.

He was the youngest of five children in a close-knit family. His father had worked at the Trepca mine until he lost his job, and then he scrambled for any job he could find—from installing heating systems to serving lunches at the downtown Mother Teresa Center. Fisnik tried to help make money for the family by selling gum, lighters, and cigarettes outside his apartment building.

On April 14, 1999, the family was ordered by Serbs to leave their small apartment. As they did, the men were pulled out of the line, and the women and children were told to keep walking. As Fisnik, his mother, and sisters continued down the street, they heard the gunshots. Every day since then, Fisnik has walked past the place in front of his apartment where his father, uncle, and cousin were killed.

The best times with Fisnik were on the basketball court. In terms of skill, he ruled, and we all knew it. But what was just as admirable was his teamwork. Rather than taking the winning shot, he would often toss the ball to someone else. He included everyone in the action—even me. "Come on, Teacher," he would say, "you know what to do." Fisnik loved a challenge. He worked hard to master his skills, and several years before graduating, he was drafted as the youngest player ever to play on Mitrovica's professional basketball team.

I cheered for him at his games. He cheered for us at the learning center by recruiting students and coming back to assist in my third- and fourth-grade English classes. A week hasn't gone by since his graduation in June 2007 (with bodyguards and cameraman!) that Fisnik hasn't texted or called.

"Teacher," he always begins. "How are things going?"

On a recent Mothers' Day he sent a note. "I'm writing to you because in the time I met you, you were not just my teacher, but you were for me everything like my mom and my best friend whom I have forever. I learned a lot of things from you that I need most in my life. I will never forget you. I want the best of the best for you, my mom."

When we opened the House of Laughter, my 10-year-old daughter tucked her sandy blonde hair under a clown's hat and helped pass out balloons to our visitors. One of those visitors was a thirteen-year-old boy named Lavdim.

Eight years later, I sat next to Lavdim as we drove out of Prishtina toward Mitrovica. A lot of things had changed during those years we had known each other. For one thing, Lavdim was sitting in the driver's seat, and I was in the passenger seat. It used to be the other way around. He was no longer the quiet, shy thirteen-year-old I had greeted at the grand opening of the House of Laughter. Now he was a twenty-one-year-old man with conviction and courage. Another change was that I used to ask him the questions; on this day, he wanted to ask me a question. He took a deep breath. In that breath, my mind raced across years of memories and stories.

When Lavdim was five years old, his father was dismissed from his position as an electrician at a large factory as part of President Slobodan Milosevic's cut in employment for Albanians. Lavdim's family learned to not waste anything. If they needed a notebook, they would make one from a paper flour sack. Seven years later, during the war in April 1999, Lavdim's father was shot and killed while trying to get food for his family. When the family and other villagers were evacuated, Lavdim's uncle and brother hid under piles of clothing crammed into a wagon, while Lavdim and his mother and sister sat on top. They came to the inspection point where Serbian soldiers were pulling men away, but they were allowed to pass without unloading the wagon.

After the war, Lavdim's mom heard about the House of Laughter. She knew how much her son wanted to learn English, and she encouraged him to attend. There was no money for a bus from their home three kilometers away, so Lavdim walked. He came faithfully, was respectful, and learned English so well that, at the age of fourteen, he became a translator for visitors at the House of Laughter.

My memories raced across all the fun summers we spent in the Rugova Mountains, where Lavdim saw how a family works together. He started as a camper—gathering firewood, setting up tents, cooking over the open fire, hiking to the lake, and cleaning the campsite. Over the years he qualified for the Leadership Educational Development program. One lesson Lavdim learned in those years was that if you want to lead you must serve.

I admired the way Lavdim took care of his mom and sisters, living out his convictions with a tender heart. Because there had been no work before and after the war, he was frugal. When his friends went out for coffee, he headed home. He saved money to pay for eye surgery, his driver's training, and his passport.

And I couldn't help but observe how Lavdim treated Lydia. He had always been her best friend. When she needed counsel about cultural issues, he was there for her. But it wasn't until several years later that *she* realized how much he meant to *her*. Now they were graduates of the House of Laughter and had completed their first year at the American University of Kosovo.

As we were riding along with Lavdim at the wheel, my mind caught up to the moment.

"What did you want to ask me?" I asked him.

"I love Lydia," he said. "I want to love her and take care of her the rest of my life. May I marry your daughter?"

Since the House of Laughter opened on September 15, 2001, hundreds of young people have walked through its doors and into our lives. "Teacher," they still call me, but I've been learning from them too.

Through my students I've seen God shape individuals into a family, and I've seen that a family can't survive without grace. We make mistakes, we learn, we grow, and we forgive.

From kids who had lived through crisis, I learned that faith helps us take the first step and keep going—even when nothing makes sense, humanly speaking.

Turning serious moments around by having fun, I've seen, brightens the day for people having a hard time, and it hints at better things to come. Laughter is a gift, a reminder that God "gives us richly all things to enjoy."

And I learned about the value of friendship.

Reflecting back to my wedding day, I knew I had married my best friend. When God took Lydia's dad to heaven before she had a chance to meet him, I prayed that one day He would give her a very special young man.

He answered that prayer!

What a privilege it has been to have a small part in the life of my daughter's best friend.

In 2009, after eight incredible years, we held our last graduation at the learning center. During the first six years, we had focused on the needs of those who had suffered loss during the war. In 2007, we expanded our outreach to the general public, and though classes filled up right away, parents and children continued to come daily, seeking to register. It was time to take another step.

The House of Laughter was ready for another graduation—its own.

13

HOPE AND A FUTURE

"For I know the plans I have for you," declares the Lord,
"plans to prosper you and not to harm you,
plans to give you hope and a future."
Jeremiah 29:11

I love adventure, but that doesn't mean I am not afraid when it comes my way. For example, repelling in the mountains of Rugova is a lot of fun, but that first step backwards off the cliff is the toughest. Before taking that step my legs shake and my heart pounds. I hesitate and then step off. After that it is a blast.

Proposing the Kosovo Leadership Academy was one of those frightening first steps. In order to grow as an educational entity in Mitrovica, we needed a stable facility. The House of Laughter began on land leased to us through 2008, but in August of 2006, city officials asked us to move in order to allow use of the facility for a public medical school. We rented the second floor of another building through the next year, and we moved again in 2007, when the city offered another facility free of charge. We were informed that the Kosovo Security Forces would be taking that property at the end of 2009.

On a larger scale, the needs and structure of Kosovo's educational system are changing. On February 17, 2008, Kosovo declared its independence, having survived the conflict in 1999 and ten years of controversy. Leaders of this new country with a youthful population (almost half are eighteen or younger) are making education a priority. Government officials set goals to reduce the number of school shifts by providing more school buildings and to improve the quality of teaching through training and curriculum changes.

The Kosovo Leadership Academy would help with these reform efforts, we proposed. It would operate as a university prep school designed to prepare future leaders. Character training would be woven through the curriculum. Rather than being a supplementary program, it would qualify graduates to apply for universities in Kosovo and internationally. We hoped to enroll approximately 500 students.

Kosovo's cultural context offers a rich opportunity to promote high-quality education based on biblical principles. Our eight years with the House of Laughter gave us the chance to build community relationships, demonstrate changed lives in our students, and gain credibility as educators. Our proposal was met with complete support. The local government leaders granted us 2.47 acres of land to build a school they believed would improve their city and country.

Bill Hanson, the executive director of ABWE's Project Office, commissioned an educational assessment for the school. In February 2009, Mr. John Hess and Dr. Stephen Gruber, education professors from Cedarville University, flew to Kosovo. They studied our objectives, curriculum, and ground plans. They met with our steering committee and city officials. Later we received their document of approval for the Kosovo Leadership Academy.

I knew this school was what Mitrovica desperately needed, and I was confident that this was the direction God wanted me to go. I thought I was ready for this adventure. I thought I had faith that God would provide every dime for the project. So my next goal was to move forward in the preparation.

Another exciting educational adventure was happening in the lives of Lydia and Lavdim as they prepared to start classes at Cornerstone University in Grand Rapids, Michigan. Both of them had completed general education classes at the American University of Kosovo, a branch of the Rochester Institute of Technology. They were eager to continue their education at Cornerstone, where Lydia would major in secondary English education and Lavdim would finish his business administration degree. Both had declared a minor in Teaching English to Speakers of Other Languages (TESOL), to help students in the new academy when they came back. We arrived in Grand Rapids in late August, three weeks before classes started, and dropped Lavdim off for soccer camp. That's when he met the university president, Dr. Joseph Stowell, who came out on the soccer field to greet the team during one of their early training sessions.

Lydia and I made a quick road trip to visit family in Michigan and Ohio. We got back to Cornerstone in time for orientation and to set up Lydia's dorm room. I was excited, *of course*. But I also knew that the last item on the parent to-do list was getting closer. It was time for me to let go. For nineteen years Lydia and I had been together. She had been more than a daughter; she had been my friend, my sidekick, my teammate. The morning I was scheduled to leave, Lydia and Lavdim met me on campus before their classes started. We talked, hugged, and cried together, and then said goodbye. I drove to Ohio to return my dad's car. My parents took me to the airport, where we said our goodbyes. It was a long, lonely flight back to Kosovo.

I arrived back in Mitrovica, telling myself to get it together. I had a big job to do. While in the US I had met with several educational consultants, and I was eager and ready, I thought, to chart a direction for the Kosovo Leadership Academy on the home field.

But God had other plans. He enrolled me in another school. One where I was the student.

It all started with a phone call Sunday evening, October 25, 2009. It was Lavdim's sister—my friend Arta. We had just had dinner together four nights before, so I was surprised when she said she was having severe headaches and needed a ride to the hospital Monday morning. I was free, so I picked up Arta and Naim, her husband, at six in the morning and we headed to the Prishtina Hospital. None of us was expecting what lay ahead.

Arta walked into the hospital doubled over and throwing up into a plastic bag. After a long wait, while the receptionist sat behind his desk reading the newspaper, Arta was admitted into the hospital. Her headaches did not improve, and two days later, after being given a spinal tap, she was sent in an ambulance to a private hospital for a brain scan. Her husband and I went too, riding in the back with Arta. Everything went smoothly during the brain scan, and we started the ten-minute drive back to the Prishtina hospital.

However, while pulling out of the driveway, the driver ran over the steep curb, causing all of us to pitch forward, tumbling out of our seats. The back of the ambulance began filling with smoke. When other drivers kept honking and motioning him over, the ambulance driver finally stopped and got out. The back right wheel was ready to fall off. The driver called the hospital and asked someone to send another ambulance, which arrived an hour later. It took that long because the replacement ambulance stalled every two or three minutes on the way. Then it broke down completely. Frustrated, Naim and I ran up and down the street trying to find a van with a driver willing to take us to the hospital. A construction worker on break helped place Arta into the back of his work van, which was cleaner than the ambulance we were in before, and he took us back to the hospital.

I was beginning to see life from a Kosovar's perspective. There are no simple, quick tasks.

Arta's brain scan showed a tumor that needed to be removed. She was transferred to the surgery department where she shared a room with three other patients. The room was dark and dingy, with cockroaches crawling up the walls.

Wednesday night I went home and began to study. My medical education so far had only produced certificates in first aid and CPR. So that night I studied brain tumor symptoms, diagrammed the brain from different angles, investigated the types of tumors as well as risk factors, and wrote out twelve questions to ask the surgeon. I finished at about two in the morning. I was ready.

We were back at the hospital by 8 a.m.—waiting. When the surgeon walked by, I asked if I could ask him a few questions when he had some free time. I waited until he called me into his office. After introducing myself, I explained why I was there.

"Do you have any medical background?" he immediately asked.

"No sir, but I think it's impor—" He didn't let me finish.

"Get out of here. I don't need to talk to you." He rudely pointed to the door.

I walked out respectfully because I knew he would be operating on Arta's brain, and I did not want to offend him. But I was angry, beginning another lesson in what it felt like to be a Kosovar. In the next few days I watched doctors and nurses treat patients and their families as though they had no value; I saw fights between security guards and family members in the hospital corridors. Then I began to see a vicious cycle. Average Kosovars have no health education, so they run to the doctor for everything and demand to know what is going on. Doctors and nurses, on the other hand, are swamped with work and do not have the time to discuss basic health issues with the patients. I began to see that I was just another nuisance, just like everyone else, and this frustrated me.

Arta's surgery was successful, but the diagnosis was not good. She was diagnosed with choriocarcinoma. This meant she would need chemotherapy at the hospital six hours a day, three days a week. I knew that besides coping with the news about his wife's diagnosis, Naim was struggling with how to manage her treatment. He had no car. The hospital was over an hour away. Since I was not on a regular teaching schedule at the moment, I had some flexibility. Besides that, Arta is a gracious, generous young mother with the gift of hospitality, and I was thankful for the chance to help by becoming her caregiver. For the next three months, my office was at the bedside of women in a hospital room, where I plugged in my laptop and got to work. I didn't realize God was about to use it as my classroom.

Sitting next to the bed of a loved one diagnosed with cancer puts a new perspective on life. Cancer is no respecter of persons:

rich, poor, young, old, professional, unprofessional, educated, non-educated. I watched an Albanian nurse administer chemo to a Serbian patient and listened as the two conversed politely. It doesn't matter where we are from, the brand of our clothes, or the size of the paycheck that arrives at the end of the month. When life is at stake, people realize relationships are more valuable than anything else in this world. The husband of one of the patients in Arta's room sold his land to pay for one chemotherapy treatment.

Most days I didn't sit still for long. The nurses moved nonstop, and they asked me to help. I learned to hook and unhook infusions, and to take blood pressure readings. I emptied urinary drainage bags. I was sent on errands, like delivering specimens to the lab for biopsy. And I watched as up to nine ladies—some lying two to a bed since there were only six beds—received chemo treatments.

I was touched by the comfort and acceptance the ladies and their loved ones shared with each other. I watched three or four cancer patients sit in a little circle on their beds and laugh as they shared their stories. One lady baked a cake for everyone in the room. When one patient needed a smaller IV tube (they are responsible for bringing many of their own supplies), another patient pulled one from her purse to help. When one of the women needed water, the son of another patient bought a big bottle of water with plastic cups for everyone.

I also learned how vulnerable people are without education. They believe what they're told without questioning it. I heard one lady say that someone she knew had been cured by drinking a teaspoon of airline fuel every day. The others all grabbed their pens and scrap paper to jot down the phone number of the place where they could buy this miracle working airline fuel.

Outside that room it was survival of the fittest. It seemed the strongest and richest won. Standing in line for routine tasks resembled being driven in a herd of cattle. Pushed from every direction, one day I decided to rely on my basketball rebounding skills. God created elbows for a good reason, I thought. If I threw my left elbow back I could keep that guy shoving from behind at a safe distance, and by blocking the space in front with my right arm and elbow I could stop all those people cutting in front of me. After holding this pose for 45 minutes, I was finally at the window. The lady told me I was at the wrong window. The one I wanted, she said, was on the other side of the room. When I went to that window, the man sent me back to the line I was just in.

After dropping Arta off at the front door every day, I would take my car around back to park. At first the guard at the back entrance would stand there, making me wait in freezing weather while he let others who slipped him a bribe walk in. I wouldn't give in to that, but I discovered that when I started carrying my computer bag instead of coming with my red backpack, he allowed me to walk right through, no questions asked. So from then on, I carried that computer bag, no matter what was in it.

I struggled while sitting in this new classroom of life. I had come to Kosovo with an established identity as director of a learning center, with the goal of helping others. That had brought with it some innate respect and helped me shape the environment in which I worked. Now I didn't know who I was. At best, I was an observant bystander.

My greatest frustration was that nothing was happening with the Kosovo Leadership Academy. I sat at my computer, working through every detail I could think of, from mission statement to number of chairs we would need to zoning issues. I wrote out cognitive, social, physical, emotional, and moral goals.

But I was afraid it was just going to turn into a big notebook to put on my shelf—plans that would end up buried under financial roadblocks. I feared that insufficient funds would cause officials here to withdraw the land. This would not only be frustrating but it would also be humbling. *I may be an educator*, I thought as I sat in a cold hospital room, *but I am not a good fund-raiser*.

While sitting between Arta's bed and the big window, I wrote this in my notebook.

February 2, 2010:

"Am I a fool? Will I be on the list of failures? Am I one that people will point to and say, 'She gave false hope. She did not keep her promise'? Have I lost my credibility? I thought the next step would be the Kosovo Leadership Academy. I thought God would provide the funds. I thought a lot of people were excited and would step up and join the team. What has happened? Nothing. All the networking—the communication—has gone nowhere. Where am I now? I am completely outside my profession. I have spent more time in the hospital than in my apartment. I have no money to rent a place for school. I have no money to pay a staff. Here I sit. It seems everything I dreamed about was just a dream. I will disappoint a lot of people. Maybe it would be better for me to live among strangers and just work for the clothes on my back and a piece of bread a day. No more dreams or visions. Dreams become reality for others with more faith, others more pleasing to God."

Little did I realize that even as I was typing those words things were happening. Work was being done, and that work was in me—the kind you might miss unless you're forced to sit still and think for a while. I thought I was ready to start a school as an educator and instead God was giving me an education. My complete concentration up to that point had been on leadership. I had read every book I could get my hands on about leadership, books like *The 21 Indispensable Qualities of a Leader* by John Maxwell.

During my devotional times, I began to focus on verses like these:

> *2 Chronicles 16:9: "For the eyes of the Lord range throughout the earth to strengthen those whose hearts are fully committed to him."*
>
> *2 Chronicles 20:15: "Do not be afraid or discouraged because of this vast army. For the battle is not yours, but God's."*
>
> *James 5:16: "The prayer of a righteous man is powerful and effective."*

I began to realize, though, that my focus was on myself. God used another book I was reading, *Following Christ* by Joseph Stowell, to help me realize that I was reading the Bible and praying with the intent of getting God to do what I wanted Him to do. I began asking God what He wanted me to do—and who He wanted me to be.

On April 1, 2010, I wrote in my journal:

> *"I am first and foremost a follower. I am here to do the will of my Savior."*

On April 18, 2010, I added this note:

> *"Today I had a little lesson in following. I was almost to the house where our Sunday morning meeting would start in thirty minutes when the neighbor across the street called out to me. 'Hey, will you help us plant these onions?' I thought he was joking, but I saw his elderly parents plant-*

ing onion bulbs. And then I thought of Christ's example. He helped others on the Sabbath and was ticked at the religious leaders who were always in church but couldn't care less about the people outside the church. All I could think was, How is this man going to know what Jesus is like if all I do is say 'hello' on my way to and from church? He needs to see Christ's love in action. I climbed over the fence and started planting onions; an hour later we finished. I invited my neighbor to join us on Sundays. I don't know if anything will happen because of planting onions, but I do know it was fun being Jesus' hands today."

What did I learn during those months of frustration and discouragement while I asked God, "What is going on in Arta's life? And in mine?" I was reminded that people are much more important than projects. I learned how to pray fervently and without ceasing as I begged God for Arta's life and health. My prayers focused on God and others. I saw that leadership starts with following. And if following Christ is simply about what I do and where I do it—well, that would be easy. We all know how to play that game. But the hard part is that it's about who I am when no one is watching.

There were other changes happening too.

In late April I flew to the US, and after a few visits with friends, drove to Grand Rapids to pick up Lydia and Lavdim, who had just finished their first year of classes at Cornerstone University. For the next five weeks, we traveled over 7,000 miles, sharing with fellow believers the future ministry of the Kosovo Leadership Academy. And then we drove to Port Huron, Michigan, near the small town where Ed and I had lived the year before Lydia was born. It was time for a wedding!

Lydia married her best friend, Lavdim Musliu, on June 12, 2010. The outdoor ceremony was hosted by Ed's brother, Jack Hennesey. Jack and his wife, Karen, opened up their beautiful, gardened backyard where we set up a white tent and latticework platform. As mother of the bride, I welcomed our guests with a word of reflection. Twenty years ago, almost to the day, Lydia's father went to heaven. He would have been thrilled to celebrate the wedding of his daughter to her best friend, a young man who had also lost his father. Pastor Eric Mounts prayed as we began. Bill Prime, our teammate from Kosovo, conducted the service, and his wife, Carol played the piano. Among the family and guests was one of our other House of Laughter graduates, Kujtim, who was now studying in Chicago and had come to Michigan to celebrate with his old friends.

It was a lot easier to fly back to Kosovo this time than it had been the year before. Lavdim and Lydia came over after their honeymoon to spend time with Lavdim's family. His sister, Arta, was still in treatment for cancer but was doing better. In September Lydia and Lavdim went back to school, and so did I. Although we hadn't started construction of the academy, I wanted to keep momentum going. So I started a pilot program with sixty-five students.

Then, in April 2011, we watched as God changed our plans again. Several ABWE staff members came to Mitrovica to negotiate the next step of the Kosovo Leadership Academy. We flew Lavdim over to join the conversation as a Kosovar citizen and a potential future administrator for the school. The mayor of Mitrovica welcomed us to his office and introduced his Director of Education. We shared our vision to enhance education in Mitrovica through the Kosovo Leadership Academy. But our vision was more than a facility. We explained the ways we wanted to serve the community through sports and drama, strengthen education throughout Kosovo with teachers' training, and eventually improve the economy by incorporating a STEM (Science, Technology, Engineering, Math) program into the school. However, a crucial requirement was a long, secure lease.

The mayor explained the typical municipal lease is for ten years. However, with a few key signatures, he felt confident he could get at least a forty-year lease from the local municipality.

The mayor then turned and spoke to his director, who got up and left the room. He came back with a piece of paper that the mayor spread out on the table between us. With increasing excitement in his voice, the mayor showed us the plan the city had drawn for a major project to be located on prime real estate. It featured a botanical park with a playground, amphitheatre, and miniature golf course. The second part of the project was to add a university in the future. The third was a school for students in grades 1–12. After hearing our educational vision for Mitrovica, he told us he would like that school to be the Kosovo Leadership Academy. We would still be responsible for our own construction costs, as before, but we could build on part of this property. It was an amazing offer. Expressing our thanks, we left the meeting with the potential of a six-acre grant in the heart of the city.

Years ago I asked myself a question: *Can I trust God with the journey even if I can't see the map?* Today I know the answer, *Yes, I can!* He is trustworthy and faithful. I have a lot of work ahead of me, but doors are open for the next chapter in the adventure of hope that God has written for me.

REFLECTION

I walk down the sidewalks of Mitrovica, just as I have since I came ten years earlier. It really does feel like home now. Friends stop to talk. And kids walking down the street still call me "Teacher." Some ask when the new school will open. And others, my former House of Laughter students, get a little more personal. They look me right in the eye, smile, and ask, "When can we have coffee?"

I came here as a single mom with a ten-year-old daughter.

My husband, Ed, died five months before Lydia was born, at the age of twenty-six. In the hard days that followed, I asked God to guide me to a role in life that I might not have had before. In those lonely nights as a young mother rocking her baby to sleep, I asked God to hold her as only a father can. God's care for the fatherless and widows became more than a Bible verse, more than a promise; it became our reality. And as our journey of grace continued, I began to hear an answer to my prayer. God led us, one step at a time, from America to Peru to Albania—and then, as single mom and fatherless child, to connect with survivors of war in Kosovo.

And He also placed in my heart a passion for education.

We are excited about the next chapter, the Kosovo Leadership Academy. What an incredible opportunity! I remember when Lydia and I first looked at a concrete slab lying in the dust among a pile of bricks in Kosovo and heard that this would become the new learning center. Eight years and hundreds of students later, it was easy to say, "Miracles really do happen!" I remember the day I looked around the House of Laughter and asked myself what it would take for us to provide more than a supplement to kids' education. What would it take to design a curriculum and facility that would not only qualify our students for university work, if they chose that path, but also prepare them to be leaders in their new nation? How could we support their potential to improve the economical, environmental, and spiritual conditions they faced? Could that happen?

Take the first step. A step of faith. I've heard God encourage me to do that many times. Perhaps you have too. Maybe that means stepping away from the casket of one you love and trusting that you will make it through that day. Maybe it means giving God your dreams for the future and trusting Him with the result. And maybe it's giving your time and energy for someone else, and trusting that it makes a difference.

My heart overflows with gratitude for the love and support of family and so many friends who have come to help us. Their lives are woven into the miracle God continues to unfold.

We're still a work in progress. What God is doing here is beyond my ability to describe or even imagine. It can't be contained in a story that happened a while ago and is over. It's happening now.

Take the first step of faith, I reminded myself before sharing the incredible dream of the Kosovo Leadership Academy. *And then trust God with the details.*

"When you don't see His plan," people around me sang at Ed's funeral. "When you can't trace His hand . . . ."

I wasn't singing then, but I can now. "Trust His heart."

About the Author

Rebecca Baker teaches and directs in the theater program at Cedarville University. She is also a licensed speech and language pathologist, specializing in professional voice. Rebecca loves to connect with her community through theater, and has acted in over a dozen shows. She helps lead the drama ministry at Southgate Baptist in Springfield, Ohio, and has been part of mission trips to the House of Laughter in Kosovo. Her first film acting role was as Maria in *Hudson Taylor*. Rebecca and her husband, Wes, have four children—Vanessa, Nathan, Kati, and Elizabeth.

Note to the Reader

The publisher invites you to share your response to the message of this book by writing Discovery House Publishers, P.O. Box 3566, Grand Rapids, MI 49501, U.S.A. For information about other Discovery House books, music, videos, or DVDs, contact us at the same address or call 1-800-653-8333. Find us on the Internet at http://www.dhp.org/ or send e-mail to books@dhp.org.